W9-AUK-152

BETWEEN FANTASY AND TUSCANY

For Mark,

You are an unexpected
but very welcome link —

Best wishes always,

Susan Brassfield
21 August 2017

BETWEEN FANTASY AND TUSCANY

Susan Braggiotti

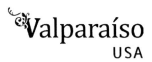

Valparaíso

USA

Number 1 in the Valparaíso Narrative Collection
Directed by Gordon E. McNeer

Cover photo, Terry C. Bird, copyright 2017

First Edition: April 2017

© Susan Braggiotti

© Valparaíso Editions USA, LLC
POB 1729. Clayton, GA 30525 USA
www.valparaisoeditions.us

ISBN: 978-0-9988982-0-9

Printed in the United States of America

All rights reserved. No part of this book may be reproduced in any form or by any electronic or mechanical means, including information storage and retrieval systems, without permission in writing from the publisher, except by a reviewer, who may quote brief passages in a review. Scanning, uploading, and electronic distribution of this book or the facilitation of such without the permission of the publisher is prohibited. Please purchase only authorized electronic editions, and do not participate in or encourage electronic piracy of copyrighted materials. Your support of the author's rights is appreciated. Any member of an educational institution wishing to photocopy part or all of the work for classroom use or in an anthology should send inquiries to:

Valparaíso USA, POB 1729, Clayton, GA 30525 USA

Flight to Tuscany

Weary from demandings and deceit, one simply opted out
To quiet Tuscany where trivia cannot abide
And Umbrian skies bring sincere smiling eyes.
She found a long-neglected farmhouse dismally alone,
Four thick stone walls, no roof nor floors.
Even the steps to outside loggia a shambles.
But to her sight this casa (circa 1700) seemed
Rough marble a sculptor might study to find a hero
Or an angel to be brought out, released.
Could that old ruin be a sun-brightened home, red-tiled
Roof and casement windows colorful with flowers—
Whole-truth beauty and contentment at a glance?
Now self-fulfilled by meaningful creativity,
Her hands made strong, heart made deeply glad,
She adopts "Il Poggetto," both name and place,
And happily calls "Buon giorno" in welcoming greetings.
Wise old oliveto trees are nurtured back to radiance
And fields of bronze-green glistening vineyards
Again breathe fruitfully in the refreshing air
Which sweeps the fragrant valley and gently stirs her hair.

Ernest L. Snodgrass

TABLE OF CONTENTS

1. IL POGGETTO

The ferryboat was taking us from the island of Capri to the romantic seaport of Positano on the Amalfi coast. It was early September, when the days are clear, dry, and hot. The sun reflected off the calm Tyrrhenian Sea, the white stucco houses, the oiled sunbathers, and shone with such intensity as if to mock the imminent arrival of wet, windy autumn.

Ciro and I were lunching informally on the *terra cotta* tiled *terrazzo* of one of the bougainvillea-bedecked villas, invited by way of Gina, my husband's charming but spoiled sister. She had her Sicilian lover in tow and brought along our mutual Tuscan friend, Raffaella.

Intelligent, knowledgeable, multilingual, and cosmopolitan, Raffaella, in her late 60s, had the energy and drive of an ambitious 25-year-old. She was feisty. Perhaps her mostly Russian blood gave her these qualities, but I suspect that added to them were her half-century struggle to be an honorable and accepted member of one of the oldest Florentine noble families. She had been born "in the shadow of the *Cupolone*," she boasted, but notwithstanding her merits, she had been nearly defeated by the malice of her brothers and her bad luck in marriage.

Her four children grown, Raffaella's life was beginning to settle down, and she had hopes of retiring to her country house in Tuscany. Ciro and I were thinking of buying just such a house and fixing it up, and mentioned our fantasy to her on the beach that day in Positano.

Raffaella, as always, had an idea. She talked to us as she coaxed her wet hair into its aristocratic upsweep. "There is an abandoned farmhouse near me. It is for sale, and a crook wants to buy it. If I could I would buy it for my daughter, but since I can't I would like to see friends get it. The house needs fixing up, but it's a good investment. Go see it on your drive back through Tuscany; it's near the toll road, and you don't even have to go into town. The name of the house is " Il Poggetto."

Ciro and I had been to Raffaella's country house near the village of Sarteano ten years earlier, in the late 1970's, so we had a vague recollection of the area. Several days later as we drove north towards Florence, I was surprised at my insistence that we take time to see the neglected farmhouse. Ciro liked my enthusiasm and got into the spirit of the adventure. It was a beautiful day, and we were in no hurry.

We got off the A-1 toll road at the Chiusi-Chianciano exit. It was lunchtime, so we stopped in a trattoria just off the highway. The restaurant looked like a converted farmhouse, built of stucco-covered stone. Part of the building was boarded up, leaving only the ground floor kitchen and restaurant open to the public. Across the street on an odd angle to the road was an old brick church, its squat bell tower silent, its exterior walls covered with posters advertising rock concerts from the summer season now past.

With a phone call from the restaurant, we made an appointment with the property owners to see Il Poggetto after lunch. Meals had enormous importance to my husband; he remembered the places he had been by what he had eaten there. This time it was typical Tuscan fare: a sample of antipasti; olives, *crostini*, salami, and a slice of prosciutto. The pasta course was homemade egg fettuccine *al ragù*; then there was chicken roasted with rosemary, sage, garlic, and plenty of salt, accompanied by fried potatoes and green salad that grew in a tiny plot behind the restaurant. The wine was the local white, not bottled but served *sfuso* in a ceramic pitcher. We were seated at a small white table outside in the shade of two oak trees. While we waited to be served, the nine-year-old daughter of the proprietors told us how eager she was to return to school the following week.

At 2:30, with the heat of the day beating down, Ciro drove us up the hill towards Sarteano as far as the turnoff to the farmhouse. Leaving the main road, we entered a narrow dirt trail largely used by tractors and followed its winding, dusty route for about a kilometer. Ahead on the left was Raffaella's house, so before it on the right and up a hill would be the farmhouse Il Poggetto.

As navigator, I concentrated on the road, on following directions, on looking for landmarks, not noticing the expanse of countryside. As soon as we drove up the overgrown driveway, I got out of the car to find in front of me a spectacular panorama of gnarled olive trees, regal cypresses, tidy vineyards, cultivated blonde wheat fields, cool woods, and in the distance the blue Umbrian hills hosting distant medieval villages.

Stunned by this Tuscan-Umbrian view, I was absorbed into its vast beauty, and every other thought left me. That sparkling day introduced me to its broad horizon, which in time I learned changes color and texture with the weather, the season, the hour of the day. In the near future life experiences would become thrilling, daunting, unexpected; but the tranquility of the view was always reassuring and helped keep everything in perspective. After many years, this view continues to inspire and enchant me.

Il Poggetto's owner had sent his 15-year-old son to show us around. To keep him company was his grandfather, suspicious but curious of us foreigners. He watched us out of the corner of his eye, making no effort to be friendly but acting only as civilly as needed to potential buyers.

Behind me like an afterthought was the 17th century farmhouse, or what was left of it, for the two-story house had been abandoned for over twenty years. Most of the roof was gone, letting in broad rays of sun, and the four tired stone walls were bereft of mortar.

We climbed awkwardly up the incline where a now dismantled staircase had led to the second story, which as in all these *case coloniche* was the original living quarters. Inside, the floor was so full of holes that we had to pick our way as if jumping mud puddles. Not one of the four rooms showed signs of plumbing. The heat source had been an enormous fireplace, its bricks and stone now strewn on the floor like pieces of a jigsaw puzzle. There was no electricity, the few casually strung wires having long since rotted away.

The boy had forgotten to bring the key to the long downstairs cow stall with its wooden trough, so I peered through the cracks in the rotted wood door to try and figure out the condition and dimensions of this main room. I asked the boy, "Does it have a concrete or dirt floor?" Both the boy and his grandfather simply shrugged as they didn't remember. How big was this cow stall? Well, maybe ten meters long. Ciro was already imagining it remodeled: "Do you think it might be big enough for a grand piano?" he asked me. The rest of the downstairs was not locked, and entering the cool rooms we saw reminders of the animals who had occupied them. As my eyes adjusted to the dark, I smiled to see that someone had painted the interior walls of the hen house sky blue. Some straw nests remained from when eggs had been gathered there. Along the other end of the ground floor I found two small pigsties with exterior doors a yard tall and damp, dark walls.

Back outside, September's heat demanded that all of nature rest. The air was still, no birds sang, the locusts had stopped their sawing, and farmers were snoozing behind closed shutters. I was out of sync with this mood as I hiked up my Liz Claiborne dress and began touring the property. In back of the house was an *oliveto* with elderly trees badly in need of trimming and fertilizing. Two fallow fields felt responsible to grow high weeds and self-generating barley. These made up the four and one-half acres included in the farm. Beyond the various sized oak trees that marked the property line were vineyards and olive groves belonging to others. Off to the south was a tree-covered mountain with an iron cross at its peak. The closest house, Raffaella's, looked to be about three hundred yards away, then further off were the four other neighboring farmhouses.

Il Poggetto captivated my imagination. It was beginning to feed my soul. I knew I had to have this place. It cried out for someone to take it over, to give it back its dignity and usefulness, and I wanted to be that someone. Ciro wanted to have a home in Tuscany, too, though the idea of the necessary remodel left him unenthusiastic.

A few days later, Ciro and I flew home to Florida. Il Poggetto haunted me, but I reneged on buying it. Suddenly thrown into the problems of bills due, my aging parents, rambunctious dogs, and the annual chore of resuming life at an American pace, I put Tuscany in the back of my mind.

We were living in an elite community in South Florida. Our large, modern, open house belonged to my stepson, and our friends and acquaintances were of Ciro's vintage, that is, about forty years older than I. It was 1987, and I had just turned thirty-nine when Il

Poggetto came along, offering an escape to a different world.

Finally, after a month away from Italy, I took affirmative action. Luckily, neither the crook Raffaella had mentioned nor anyone else bought the house before I could get it. The project was mine, independent of my husband, bought with my savings and in my name. Ciro wanted it that way so that he could remove himself from the responsibility of the remodel. At the time I didn't know the saying "*Chi non risica non rosica*", but it fit my attitude towards the house and life in general. It is a nonsensical way of saying, "Who doesn't take risks doesn't profit."

It wasn't as if Tuscany were totally foreign to me. Ciro had owned a villa on the Tyrrhenian Sea where I had spent several summers before we were married. Ciro himself was Florentine born, but a patriotic American. When his American grandfather first saw Ciro's smiling face, he said, "What a cheery little fellow." With that remark, he could not help but be named the Italian Ciro (pronounced "Chee-ro").

Ciro influenced me with his Tuscan tastes in cooking, house decoration, and lifestyle. My Italian was slow in coming, despite my musician's ear, but the little I knew would help in my project. After my first trip to Italy, I had taken a night school grammar course and studied vocabulary on my own. I had no Italian blood and with red hair certainly didn't look Italian. The Latin enthusiasm and sometimes boisterous behavior were foreign to my staid upbringing. But perhaps it was just this uninhibited exuberance of the Tuscan people that attracted me to them. Owning property in Italy seemed a natural step to take, a way of asserting my long lost independence.

But how was I to buy the house? I was in Florida, and Il Poggetto was in Tuscany.

Raffaella offered to get involved. I had known her and her children for twelve years, and though we were not close friends, she had been the one to tell us about Il Poggetto, and her country house was just next door. Having remodeled her own place, she knew the red tape and was someone who thrived on tackling bureaucratic snafus. In truth, she wanted to be influential in the rebuilding of Il Poggetto as she still harbored hopes of getting it for her 23-year-old daughter, assuming that sooner or later I would get discouraged and give up on the project.

To allow her the authority to buy the house in my name, I had to give her an Italian Power of Attorney from the Consulate in Miami. With that document, Raffaella freely chose a Roman attorney to prepare the real estate contract and to negotiate terms of the sale. She warned, "We have to offer full price or the crook will come in and offer more." She needed funds up front, which I began wiring by the thousands to a bank in Sarteano. Then at one point, she wrote, "Why don't you put the house in my daughter's name, with the agreement that you and Ciro can come and stay in it all you want?" From that moment I no longer trusted her, but being fully involved in representing me, I couldn't suddenly pull back without losing the whole deal. Finally, after two months of long-distance phone calls, wires, letters, and transfers of funds, Raffaella wrote to us in less-than-perfect English: "As of today, Susan is the righteous owner of Il Poggetto." It was early December, and we had been negotiating since October. The cost of the 1400 square foot house and its acreage: $27,000.

During that winter period of anticipation, Raffaella went about trying to find a retired mason who would be willing to begin the remodeling. She knew that we wanted the work done as cheaply as possible, and she herself had the reputation of being a champion *lira* pincher. A retired mason meant working al *nero* with no taxes involved on either side. The workman would receive an hourly wage of about $10.00 plus costs for materials. "He'll work *pian piano*," Raffaella explained, meaning quietly, slowly, calmly, finishing the house the following year sometime.

Once the property was mine, from faraway Florida I began drawing floor plans without knowing dimensions or even the number of existing rooms. I had only my memory of that hot September day when we couldn't even get into the cattle stall downstairs.

Because of the large fireplace upstairs, I envisioned an eat-in country kitchen with a new fireplace going through to a cozy sitting room, then two bedrooms and back-to-back baths. Downstairs would house our dovetailed grand pianos in a formal living room made from the cattle stall, plus an entry and another bedroom with bath.

From my Florida view of thick water oaks, citrus trees, and a flat, scrubby terrain, I dreamed of a Tuscan garden with cypress trees, a magnolia, pots of geraniums, lilies of the valley, various colored rose bushes, and a fragrant herb garden with basil, oregano, mint, thyme, sage and rosemary.

Luckily, as the *pian piano* pace would have taken years, Raffaella couldn't convince any workman to take on the remodeling project. Instead, she hired at lowest bid a local contractor. As work began in March, we arranged with Raffaella to stay in her country house from April 2 until June 10 when the rebuilding of my house was scheduled to be completed. We closed up our Florida home, expecting to return in the fall to spend the winter months. Our ideal was six months here, six months there.

2. WORK BEGINS

Because Raffaella had hired a contractor and work had begun at Il Poggetto, we arranged to fly from 80-degree Florida to the 50-degree weather in Tuscany on the second of April. Raffaella met us at Rome's Leonardo da Vinci airport in her chugging diesel Fiat station wagon. In red wool pants, parka and gloves, Raffaella greeted us with, "It's very unseasonable; usually it's warm and spring-like by this time of year." We packed aboard our six suitcases, two bulging briefcases of piano music, and my mutt Puff. Ciro sat in front with Raffaella, I in back, glad to be where I could pretend not to hear them.

As Raffaella drove north, she talked incessantly to Ciro and honked the horn periodically like a nervous cough. Ciro's Italian was a bit rusty, so mostly he just agreed with her: "*Si, si, ho capito.*" The early signs of spring green around Rome disappeared and the sky darkened. After an hour and a half, finally Raffaella turned the car into the muddy dirt road I remembered as being dusty. Earth, trees, and sky blended into a brown-grayish gloom, and on the peak of Monte Cetona with the cross on top, snow clung stubbornly. One promise of spring interrupted the dreary scene:

the early green wheat, only inches tall, dotted some of the distant fields.

The weather, though disappointing, did not dispel my excitement nor lessen my fear – fear of the unknown. My lack of confidence, understandable because of my naïveté, inexperience, and limited Italian, would become my nemesis.

We drove into Raffaella's carport. Her house had been a farmhouse similar to Il Poggetto before she had got hold of it some twenty years earlier. She had added on, bit-by-bit, bedrooms, bathrooms, a third story, a second kitchen, two loggias, and a swimming pool. The house became something of a maze; later I learned that my workmen called it a whorehouse as it was bedroom-bath, bedroom-bath, one after the other. To add to the confusion were objects from her extensive travels and the accumulation of her four children's personal belongings stored there.

Raffaella showed us our room – our home for the next two months. While we were assigned one bedroom and bath on the ground floor plus use of the upstairs kitchen and sitting room, we would have the run of the place as Raffaella spent most of her time at her apartment in Rome. For lunch, she served us some pasta with commercially prepared meat sauce and quick-thaw Cordon Bleu. Unlike Ciro and me, she had no time or patience for food preparation. After lunch, Ciro, Raffaella with her two dachshunds, Puff, and I walked up to see my house.

At Il Poggetto, the driveway had been graded and gravel laid over the mud. Around the house where there had been thick brambles and high grass, the grader had cleared all growth, making the house dominate the property, despite that the *oliveto* in back was on a higher level. The only trees adjacent to the building were a traditional lone, proud cypress off to one side and at the top of the driveway, a fig tree struggling to survive.

As work had begun in March, I was encouraged to find scaffolding on the front of the house and men rebuilding the roof.

My contractor was a local man, fifty and potbellied, who talked in such fast dialect that there was no hope of my understanding him, a fact that helped him in what I learned was his constant endeavor to cheat me. His nickname was Gattone, "Big Cat", as he looked like a wildcat that had been stuffed into a pair of jeans. He greeted us unctuously; then, to make himself appear important, he began bossing in a staccato shout the six or seven workmen under him. He began telling us how he would like to "beautify" the house inside by hanging mirrors and chandeliers.

I was impressed with the speed at which Gattone worked, though. It was he himself I found on the job when I walked up to the house the next morning. Wearing a bright red sweater, he was on the roof, mounting the *terracotta* tiles. On April 3, he had laid four of the thigh-shaped tiles in place; by 5 p.m. the following afternoon, the new roof had been completed. Too late did I realize that fast work was synonymous with haphazard work. Months later, some of the interior walls took on the unmistakable dark stain that signals a leaky roof. But in those early April days, I was thrilled with Gattone's progress.

The workmen, the men Gattone reveled in ordering around and belittling, were my salvation. These masons, true artisans, understood and appreciated tradition; they treated every ragged stone and handmade brick with respect. Considered more than laborers, in reality these *operai* had an aesthetic sense that went beyond skill, as if beauty came to them intuitively. Perhaps their sensibility was instilled from birth out of the rich natural abundance surrounding them. Their long heritage was Etruscan then Roman, with the pride and dignity those cultures boasted.

As soon as the roof had been completed, the workmen began the demolition of unusable and unsafe parts of the structure. I was eager to see rebuilding; the idea of first having to tear down had not occurred to me. As wheelbarrows full of debris were carted away and dumped by the side of the house, Ciro complained, "I thought some little man was going to do a few repairs to make the place livable. This is going to cost a fortune!"

The exterior stone was mostly porous tufa and volcanic rock, plus some blocks of unpolished, pitted travertine. The walls had to be cleaned of the old mortar and reinforced with new. Each man used a hammer and chisel to chip away by hand at the ancient walls.

A weedy incline, where the exterior stairway had once been, led to the small second story entrance *loggia*. After years of neglect, this porch had been reduced to three sagging, roofless arches. The stone and brick arches were straightened and reinforced, protected by a new roof to enclose them.

Before initiating the work upstairs, we needed to build a new staircase up to the loggia, giving second-story access to the workmen. The senior mason, Nino, had the workers clear away the debris – dirt, weeds, and broken bricks – then Nino began constructing the stairs with old brick, exactly as they had been originally. This first part of the reconstruction helped me envision what was to come – the house would rise like a phoenix, and I would fly with it into a new chapter in my life.

But my enthusiasm was dampened by Ciro and Raffaella. My dream floor plan was summarily discarded by them as impractical. "But Susan, you can't have a kitchen upstairs - we'd have to carry all the groceries up there and our guests would have to climb up to dinner," Ciro complained, then shouted, "Never!" Instead, at his and Raffaella's insistence, the plan for the interior of the house was to make a den out of the room with the fireplace (the original kitchen, upstairs of course), then put a study and two bedrooms with adjoining baths on the same floor. The rooms already existed; the only change would be to divide one room into two, to build the two baths.

Downstairs was to become a living room where the dairy cows had been sheltered, a dining room where the chickens had nested, a kitchen in what had been a storeroom, then a bath with shower and a laundry room in what had been the two pigsties. Upstairs was to be completed first so that we could move in as soon as possible, early June being our deadline. Raffaella's house was to be let beginning June 10, so we had no choice but to get out. So far, Raffaella had obtained the permit for only the upstairs renovation. Though the only staircase was exterior, I had no plans for an interior one.

Nino had begun paving the loggia with old brick in a straight pattern, whereas I had wanted a herringbone design. Gattone had ordered the nondescript pattern to save time and bricks. Nino asked me, "How do you like it?" When I murmured something about it not being the pattern I wanted, he tore up the work, saying, "This is your house, *Signora*, we're here to do as you want." Nino had more formal education than the other workmen, having completed high school, and he was older and more experienced than the others. He was a passionate music lover and passed the time at work whistling themes from the "Warsaw Concerto" or Tchaikovsky's "Nutcracker" with clear, round tones and a lovely vibrato. When he discovered that Ciro and I were musicians, he made a special effort for us. He overlooked my ignorance of Tuscan building procedures and gave me the courage to begin speaking my mind and to contradict even Gattone. In the beginning stages, Nino was the only workman whose name I knew. While I liked the *operai* and got along with them, I was terribly shy and, worse yet, miserably self-conscious of my stilted, formal, American-accented Italian.

The first two weeks at Il Poggetto brought a new roof, a repaired loggia, and my first self-assertion on the job. In those early days Ciro had been influenced by Raffaella to buy an eight-year-old sky-blue Fiat that, it turned out, stalled every time it was out in the rain. Ciro left me to do the driving with my international drivers' license. We went daily into Sarteano on errands, particularly to the grocery store, post office, and bank. Running up from the main square was the medieval *corso*, the original principal street, closed to all except delivery traffic as it was so narrow. Along the *corso* were City Hall, clothing, jewelry, and food shops, a variety store with everything from toys to Bavarian crystal, and a trattoria with six tables and a tiny kitchen with a huge window that let in the full sunlight. Ciro and I began getting acquainted with various merchants in town, especially the drunk who ran the *casalinghi* variety and house-wares shop, and the couple who owned a hardware store under a medieval archway. Ciro did the talking in these stores as I tried to learn the vocabulary for "sauce pan," "pot holder," or "paper towels." When I tried to use my Italian, Ciro would correct me impatiently. Me: *"una tegame."* Ciro: *"un tegame."* Me: *"un presso."* Ciro: *"una presa."* Me: *"asciugamani per casa."* Ciro: *"carta di casa."* Inevitably I would hear from him, "I told you that word yesterday. Why can't you remember it? How can you make such stupid mistakes! And you pronounce double consonants where there aren't any and single ones where doubles should be . . . " None of the locals in town seemed upset by the way I talked, but Ciro's impatience left me unhappily self-conscious.

While shopping left me somewhat befuddled, visits to government offices overwhelmed me by their complications. I had an inkling of what lay before me as far as actual reconstruction on my house, but I had no idea of all the paperwork, the red tape, the various permits required, and the number of people and offices I would have to visit, telephone, and visit again, all in a haphazard schedule in which appointments did not exist.

Sarteano was an undistinguished farm community of 4,300 hardworking people. The Communist Party had been in power for over forty years. Recently, there had been a Communist mayor who was highly regarded by all, even the Christian Democrats, the party of the Catholic Church and therefore furthest away from communism. Currently, a very young mayor, also Communist, ran the town with the help of his pals, most of whom were inexperienced in the duties of the offices they held.

On one of my first solo trips to town I went in jeans and a pink stadium jacket to City Hall to apply for residence. City Hall was a medieval building on the *corso*. Its unobtrusive entrance belied the several stories of offices, all housing the latest computerized equipment. In the office of statistics, a burly man with wavy white hair waited on me. As he interviewed me, I noticed behind me a slick-looking man of about 40 with very dark eyes and a trim mustache. He was wearing a black leather jacket. He hung around eavesdropping as the clerk filled out government forms about me. I didn't like the looks of what I thought for sure was a crook who kept lurking behind me, and I pretended not to notice him.

I told the gruff man waiting on me that I wanted residence in Italy only for myself, but he would not accept my request. "Usually married people live together," he concluded, so I applied for residence for Ciro as well, though he didn't want it. Having residence was important for me as the property owner because it was supposed to ameliorate various bureaucratic problems associated with rebuilding a farmhouse, plus it would give me a tax break. The clerk said that it would take several months before we would be approved as residents because the state would want to check out our pasts. He helped me fill in the necessary form: height, 163 centimeters; eyes, blue; hair, blonde, "Or even *rossicci*," he said and almost smiled, but he decided on "dark blonde" for the official form. As I finished up with this intimidating bureaucrat, the crook behind me spoke, but not to me. "Felice," he teased, "*non sei davvero felice di aiutare questa bella signora?*" Felice means "happy," and that was Mr. Grouch's given name! While Felice may have been glad to wait on the "*bella signora*" as the crook had suggested, he didn't even respond to yet another joke about his humiliating name. I tried not to smile, but I certainly relaxed, though the crook still left me feeling wary.

By mid-April we were beginning to feel settled in at Raffaella's house. Luckily, she was in Rome for long periods, leaving us on our own. While cooking, Ciro would invariably bump his head on the overhead stove hood, then hit the hood back in defense. We ate our meals – pasta at lunch, soup in the evening – in front of the large, comforting fireplace in the sitting room as Puff snoozed nearby. I enjoyed the tranquility surrounding us and began hearing birds whose songs I could not identify. As spring progressed the Italian miniature robins began moving north, but for now they were still singing their cheerful tune. I hadn't seen robins since college.

I had graduated from the Music School of Indiana University with a degree in piano performance. My ambition: to perform on stage. When I met Ciro he was a well-established pianist, his formal education coming from the Paris Conservatoire with its concentrated classical music courses. His general education left him lacking in many areas: he lamented that he had never learned long division. But he was a knowledgeable musician. We had formed a piano duo only recently. In his youth Ciro had known George Gershwin and won the composer's admiration, so we had decided to concentrate on an all-Gershwin program for which Ciro wrote the arrangements. Our forty-year age difference didn't seem to matter: I was young, talented, ambitious; he was established, experienced, but also still ambitious. I knew that he chased women, but it didn't bother me: no other woman would give him what I could. I was making myself indispensable to him, and he was providing me the career I wanted.

We had contracts for several prestigious European concerts coming up in the summer, the first to be in Chartres, France, and we were able to add more dates after arriving in Italy. We had three months to practice before the initial concert. While we had learned the program in Florida and had it in our fingers, Ciro and I both knew that regular practice was essential, so we rehearsed our Gershwin program on two rented uprights installed in Raffaella's downstairs living room. As instruments they left a lot to be desired after our two grand pianos in Florida, but we banged out Gershwin's "Concerto in F" and a "Porgy and Bess" suite as if we wanted the workmen up the hill at Il Poggetto to hear the music.

As an experienced performer, Ciro had offered me the life I wanted. His charisma and vitality made him larger than life on stage, where I had first seen him. His charm and humor flew across the footlights, and his pianistic technique put me and all who heard him under his spell immediately. When we were first introduced, his Latin sex appeal had left me feeling lightheaded. After telling me, "I'm looking forward to a nice shower after that performance," which I found provocative, he offered, "You must come to my villa on the sea in Tuscany; I'll sponsor you in a recital." It was May, and at 26 I had just planned my first trip to Europe that summer, to Spain where my brother lived. "Is Tuscany very far from Spain?" I asked naively. A few days later he wrote me a letter. "You are springtime, loveliness, and music…." With the certainty of a romantic adventure, I did go that summer and gave a solo recital in the enormous music room he had added to a modest beach house in Porto Santo Stefano. We stayed together from then on.

Like a lot of geniuses, he was impractical, irresponsible, and somewhat fickle, but his youthful enthusiasm and innocent practical jokes were fun. I had never been around such an easygoing person, for even as a child I was always trying to be "mature" and "intellectual". Ciro's appetite for life was enormous and his libido insatiable. Cooking was another of his passions, and when preparing a meal everything else was sidelined. "You answer the phone," he would tell me, "I can't talk now." (Me? I didn't even know to say "*Pronto*" on answering the phone) At lunch, eaten on his huge outdoor terrace, he would ask, "What do you want for dinner?" Then at dinner he would say, "Tomorrow morning we'll go into the port and get some fresh swordfish!" He had us taking rain baths outdoors in our swimsuits. One night we watched a late storm arrive while we sat in his music room with its huge windows, wearing our pajamas, me wrapped in his enveloping arms. He took me to the nude beach and made me feel completely comfortable in my skin. When a new wheelbarrow was delivered, he loaded me up for a ride in it through the garden. While I was taking a warm shower, suddenly he would throw cold water on me. We were allowing ourselves to be childlike, and I believe that helped us in our music, too, making it more spontaneous and energetic. His puns left everyone going "ughhhh", but they were clever: "What did one baby chick say to the other baby chick?" "Look at the orange mama laid!'" or "Where did you get your ascot?" "In the revolving door."

Fifteen years later, though, Ciro wasn't as enthusiastic about performing but instead shifted his attention to writing musical comedies. Having an agreeably subservient nature, being totally in love with him, and assuming incorrectly that he knew what he was

28

doing, I let him put me to work typing his manuscripts once, twice, six times. Gradually through our years of collaboration I began doing the editing, then the actual writing within his story lines, then became his lyricist, as I had a talent for writing words to his tunes. So my career expanded beyond piano playing into musical theater and songwriting.

Il Poggetto came along for me at just the right time. Besides our concerts, I had worked with Ciro on his various musical and theatrical projects for those fifteen years, but we had nothing to show for them except vast numbers of files, scores, and letters of rejection. Ciro was the love of my life, and I was his, but our lack of success was very discouraging to both of us. He had so little self-confidence in his musicals that he never considered them ready, constantly rewriting, adding or taking out songs, changing dialogue. He couldn't get beyond the creative and performing point into the promotional and business end.

Once finally we did present a backers' audition to some friends in Florida. Several people put $2,000 apiece towards an eventual production, the money deposited in a separate account and not touched. In the end, Ciro gave the money back, much to the surprise of the "backers."

3. GETTING ACQUAINTED

Work on Il Poggetto was interrupted for Easter. *"Non è bella la Pasqua se non goccia la frasca."* (Easter isn't beautiful unless the twig drips.) According to this aphorism my first Easter in Sarteano was beautiful, as the weather continued to be rainy and chilly. Ciro and I remained at home, as we had no social life with the local people. I didn't know what I had missed by not going into town on Easter, but later the workmen described the festivities. As morning dawned, the church bells rang with renewed energy. After a full house at morning Mass, there had been an Easter parade with the local band in blue and white uniforms leading the way informally down the main street and through the old part of town.

Easter lunch saw extended families gathered together to eat pasta *al forno* such as lasagne, milk-fed lamb called *abbacchio*, special Tuscan anise seed cookies named *brigidini*, and white cake covered with confectioner's sugar and baked in the shape of a dove. The local Chianti was pure, everyone was in a festive mood. In the afternoon friends called on one another to show off their new clothes. The men drank homemade *grappa* made from distilled grape seeds. The conversation was like a script it was full of banalities, but became heated when the men talked about the national soccer teams. "Hey, did you see that goal Maradona made yesterday?! *Incredibile!*" The housewives, relaxing in a separate room from the men, drank espresso, discussed the meal they had just served, and called out to their children playing outdoors not to get dirty. "Did you know that Angela *fa l'amore con Luca?*" (and "make love" was exactly what they do). Everyone was in an appropriately bright mood, for the Resurrection represented the beginning of good things: the revival of nature, spring, and the *bontà* of the land. Even if many of the populace were not practicing Catholics, the Church held an important part in the feeling of community, in celebrating the seasons, and in the traditions of the town.

Easter Monday, too, was a holiday: Monday of the Angel, or more simply *Pasquetta*. So the workmen had a long weekend. When they returned on Tuesday theirs was a positive attitude of "the worst is over" as far as the weather was concerned. Sinking in the mud I couldn't share their enthusiasm. "Last year we built a hotel and had snow falling on us as we hammered," Nino told me.
Gattone's presence on the property became more and more scarce. Each time I saw him I would remind him of something he had left undone, or I would complain, for example, that he was using new bricks instead of old. Finally he said, "Anything you want done, just tell Aurelio."

But which workman was Aurelio? He must be the dark-skinned one who looked to me like an Eskimo, I thought, the one so outgoing and friendly. No, he turned out to be Nuccio, Aurelio's helper. Aurelio had only recently come on the job, after the roof had been finished. At first he didn't even look at me. All the other workmen greeted me with *"Buon giorno, Signora"* in the morning and *"Buona sera"* after lunch, but Aurelio never allowed our eyes to meet. He was always working full speed, reinforcing a wall, laying bricks, and I could see that the other workers respected him. Aurelio was the *capo muratore,* the head mason second only to Nino, who was older. Aurelio certainly earned his title; he was a perfectionist in even the smallest job, hard at work by 7:30 and the last to leave after dark in the evening.

Aurelio looked to be about 45. He was muscular but slight, of average height. Being a mason, he had large, rough hands, and no weight seemed too heavy for him. It was as though his hands had outgrown the rest of him, becoming large enough to accommodate the work he required them to do. Physically he was not a stereotypical Latin: his brown hair was thinning, but he had splendid green eyes and a refined nose. He always wore a cap, a *beretto,* that he made from a brown paper bag. All the workmen wore them, partly to avoid the dirt, partly to protect themselves from the sun, and often to hide baldness.

Aurelio had spent fifteen years working as a mason in Switzerland where they called him Toscano. Because of that experience he had a more sophisticated and open view of the world than the average Sarteanan. I had noticed that one of the men often sang on the job, but it was several days before I realized that the heartfelt tenor belonged to Aurelio. He did it to help pass the time, for the others as well as for himself. He had a rich, natural voice and sang with unabashed sentiment. His love songs were full of heartbreak: "Don't think of me; continue down your path without even thinking of me. After all, there has been only a parenthesis between us." Or love overflowing: ". . . I live in your heart, you know. Anyone after you would be impossible;" or secret love: "Little boy running through my garden, little boy, you made me fall in love." Although Aurelio was shy he could overcome his timidity through his songs.

When I was on hand at the site there were always on-the-spot decisions to be made, and in my absence those decisions were made by the worker doing the job or by Gattone – if he happened to be around. It was a big mistake for me not to be at the house for longer periods of time each day. Every morning, Ciro, Puff and I would walk up to the site, greet the workmen, take a superficial look around, then after a half-hour or so would leave. Ciro always wanted me to grocery shop with him in the morning, plus there were other errands to run. He insisted that we stay together as much as possible. We would not return to Il Poggetto until after lunch, repeating the morning's brief visit, then we would go back to Raffaella's house to rehearse yet again our Gershwin program, running through it slowly and concentrating on details of certain phrases that Ciro felt didn't play right.

One morning we arrived just as a prefabricated fireplace was being installed upstairs where the old fireplace had been. Nino was on the job, whistling as usual, and was framing the fireplace with pieces of local fossilized stone, unpolished marble, and old brick. For the mantle Aurelio had found an enormous slab of travertine which had been over the front door of another abandoned farmhouse. The beauty of the piece lay in its massiveness and its irregular shape. Placed on its side, it lost its potency, but upright it was dramatic and strong. Nino began installing it on its side over the fireplace, making it into a shelf. Aurelio took me aside and said, "If you let him install that beautiful piece like that, I'll never come back here to work." That was clear incentive for me to tell Nino to rearrange the stone. Because I had been there to insist, the slab was placed upright in all its glory, and Aurelio didn't have to quit his job. Whether or not Aurelio had been serious in his threat to quit didn't matter; I wasn't going to risk losing this *operaio*.

In these old Tuscan farmhouses there were no windows or doors on the north side of the house. Being a lover of light, I wanted to add a second window in the master bedroom. "Don't do it, Signora," Aurelio advised, "when the *tramontana* blows you'll feel it." The *tramontana* is the freezing north wind that comes down from the Arctic in winter. *Tramonto* means sunset, and the wind is called *tramontana* because it is at its worst when the sun is about to set, then it usually calms down completely after sunset. The men added the window; and, of course, the wind howls through now in winter. As work progressed I learned to take the workers' advice. After all, they had years of experience behind them and I had none. Buildings, like the people, were put together differently here.

The initial stages – choosing floor tiles, light fixtures, windows, even hardware for the doors – were difficult and confusing. Not only did I not know the Italian words for these items, I didn't know the market. Did I need *semidoppio, termico,* or *antiproiettile* glass in the windows? After dismissing the need for thermal or bulletproof glass, I chose regular single panes for the upstairs. Did I want windowsills of travertine, *mattone, peperino,* or *mattonelle?* The advantage in renovating the upstairs first was that by the time I did the downstairs, I had learned the difference between brick and tile, red marble and travertine.

Most difficult of all was going against the wishes of either Raffaella or Ciro. She, having found the house and having been in on its purchase, felt not only responsible, but in charge. She would give orders to the men in front of me and without consulting me, and I was too shy and intimidated to contradict her. She had hired Gattone and had him on the job before I even knew who he was. The first thing to go was my dreamt-of floor plan. She and Ciro moved the kitchen downstairs and rearranged the rooms upstairs. As she knew a draftsman in town, her floor plan was adopted before I could learn the Italian word for floor plan: *pianta.* She insisted that the house have shutters in chocolate brown, where I had wanted forest green. "All the houses use brown in this area," she insisted, as I gazed at the green shutters on the farmhouse 300 yards off to the left of my property.

Mostly my husband was oblivious to what was going on, living in his world of music, but he would have moments of sudden interest in the house, especially if Raffaella were around. The two of them would simply ignore me, the owner. While Ciro had great charm and wit, he could be an obstinate bully about getting his way. His size in itself was intimidating: six-foot-two and 200 pounds, with broad shoulders and Germanic features inherited from his maternal side. Added to those were his inexhaustible energy and Latin appetite for arguing loudly. Because he spoke fluent Italian, the workmen took his orders seriously. Raffaella convinced him that we should put vinyl wallpaper in the bathrooms, and he dragged me to several shops to get samples and compare costs of this ugly, impractical covering. I knew that in short order the stuff would start to peel, never having looked good in the first place. In this decision I simply dragged my feet until they lost interest, Ciro and Raffaella moving on to a new project.

Ciro had some good ideas for the house, but I didn't go along with all of them, especially when he wanted to cut corners to save a few *lire*. I was dealing with something important that promised to have a long future (if not mine, at least the house's), and I didn't think being stingy was a good investment. I let Ciro have his choice in the secondhand furniture (expendable) and the pale pink color of the bedroom walls as that could be changed easily. But he would have put only a shower and no tub in the master bathroom and tiny sinks and no bidets (even though he was European) in all three bathrooms. Ciro wanted to buy floor tiles that had to be waxed, simply because Gattone had them on hand, left over from another job. I knew that I would be a slave to them, trying to keep them clean and waxed. In the end we did buy enough of them for the upstairs. Several months and much experience later, Aurelio helped me choose *monocottura* tiles for the downstairs. They needed only a simple mopping and no waxing ever.

Slowly I learned how to get my way, sometimes by putting off a decision like the vinyl wallpaper until Raffaella moved on to something else. One day on site, Raffaella ordered in front of me, "Aurelio, cut *dentini* into those wooden overhangs." Aurelio looked at me, but when I said nothing he went ahead, cutting the "teeth mark" design in the soffit beams. I still couldn't contradict her in person, but if Raffaella weren't around, I saw that my decisions were carried out.

Soon after arriving in April, Ciro and I made a visit to town to see the *geometra*, a sort of combined architect, surveyor, and law enforcer of the various permits. The *geometra* had the power to change prices set by the contractor, supposedly to protect the client, but not necessarily, if the *geometra* and the contractor were in cahoots. In my case the *geometra* was an ancient, single-toothed man named Landi whose voice trailed off at the end of every sentence as if he were expiring his last breath. "But," Raffaella said, "he's honest." She had chosen him, she said, because he was "a good, educated Catholic in a town governed by Communists." In my first meeting with Landi, I did a lot of nodding and agreeing when in reality I understood nothing of what he said: "… *per avere il permesso…Montepulciano…regionale…catasto…appalto… spazi interni…fabbricato.*" ??? Ciro sat by but didn't get much of it either, as he didn't know the technical terms Landi used. It was just as well that I didn't understand Landi's discouraging report.

Stated under the laws created by a branch of the Italian cultural ministry, or the *Belle Arti*, to protect historical buildings, I couldn't add to the volume of the house and couldn't change the general structure in any way. To add windows I needed a special permit per window, and getting a permit at all to remodel the downstairs would be tricky. Going ahead and making changes such as adding the master bedroom window was illegal, but contractors did the work anyway as permits took so long. Landi promised that he would put in the requests with the regional board. Meanwhile he made it clear that I owed Gattone *"dieci milioni di lire..."* ($8,000), partial payment for the roof, and Landi himself *cinquecentomila lire...*"($300) for services to date. A checkbook from my new account at the Monte dei Paschi Bank I had; the rest I would deal with later.

4. SIP: THE TELEPHONE COMPANY

Chilly weather continued through all of April. What looked like redbud, another reminder of my college years in Indiana, began to show bits of color, and the cherry trees bloomed timidly. It was still too early for the forsythia. The fireplace and electric blanket at Raffaella's kept us comfortable.

The men had poured the new floor upstairs and had added a wall between what were to become the guest room and the two back-to-back bathrooms. The current job was to spray plaster on the walls, a dirty task that made the rooms gray and dismal. The plaster's residue hung like fog in the damp, cold air of the house. One rainy morning I felt sorry for the five men working under such bleak conditions, so I took a jug of coffee to them. They always ate *colazione* - a sandwich and some fruit - at around 9:30, but I thought some coffee along with their food would warm them up. Each of the men had an excuse for not accepting the coffee: tall, lanky, slow-moving Fabio had liver trouble; Nuccio, (the one who looked like an Eskimo) complained of colitis; Aurelio said that coffee was bad for his heart. The only one eager for it was Gattone. He was the only one who smoked cigarettes, as well. The truth was that the men were embarrassed that I, for whom they worked and thus was their *padrona*, would go to the trouble of bringing them coffee. Although they refused it, we all felt closer from that day on, for I had demonstrated that I didn't consider myself above them. They even began swearing in front of me, apologizing at first, but I said, "I'm deaf and blind in front of you," so they bellowed away.

Swearing in Italian almost invariably had to do with taking in vain the name of the Madonna. The Madonna was a sow, the Madonna was a beast. They even called her tubercular, filthy, poisoned, and a whore. The women and men on good behavior said simply "Madonna," lingering over the n's, or "*Madonnina*," but neither of these was considered swearing. The same or similar adjectives were used with God. Once when a farmer's wife, perched on a ladder, couldn't quite reach the end of the olive branch she was picking, she cried out, "*Dio sposato!*" (God married!), certainly the worst wish to impose on the Almighty.

The phrase that I caught on to and decided I could adopt was *Dio rospo* (God is a toad). I said to the mason Aurelio, "That isn't swearing, because a toad is a creature of God." "No," he corrected, "the toad is a creature of the devil!" So I dropped that expression and exchanged it for "*Dio mostarda*" which is about as ridiculous as saying "God is chutney".

The windows and doors were ordered for the upstairs; I had decided on an iron-framed glass entrance door with a pattern of iron fleur-de-lis to serve against intruders as well as for decoration. The design helped soften the austerity of the stone walls. Actually, I ordered iron because I didn't know that I could have bought light-weight, rustproof aluminum, and a decision needed to be made.

The smithy, a young local man, came to take the measurements. Calvi, a husky, dark young man with thin lips, was shy and quiet, ingenuous, and without ambition. He seemed resigned to his lot in life and was a hard worker. A man of few words, his answer to every question was a shrug of the shoulders and a questioning tilt of the head. That physical expression remained in the vocabulary between my workmen and me. Calvi wasn't keen to do the work I required as he was in constant demand by the farmers to repair their equipment. But he was good-natured about taking on this more refined work, and the men teased and encouraged him whenever he came to the house. On his arrival one of the men would say something like, "Oh, Calvi, try not to waste too much of our time with one of your long conversations."

The upstairs windows were to be framed in wood rather than iron, as in the downstairs. I accepted reluctantly Raffaella's recommendation for a carpenter to make the windows, shutters, and built-in armoire for the master bedroom. Her carpenter had a distinguished air about him; he was young and had delicate features. He looked as if he should have been a violinist. As an artisan it was appropriate to refer to him by his surname, Damiani, rather than demote him to labor status by calling him by his first name. To say "Signor Damiani," though, would have been exaggerating his importance.

Raffaella had particular enthusiasm about this man. She faintly smiled when she referred to him. One evening as she smoked her after-dinner cigarette, she confided in Ciro and me, "You know, Damiani has a lover my age." "I wonder why?" I asked incredulously. For once she said nothing. It took me months to realize that Raffaella was Damiani's lover.

This carpenter's estimate was nearly half that of another carpenter in the area, and too late I discovered why. Certainly Raffaella would have liked to take the credit for his low estimate, but actually it was because he used cheap materials and was slapdash in his workmanship. The windows leaked air and water, and the shutters were difficult to hang as their measurements had not been taken carefully. The armoire, really a series of cupboards covering the north wall of the master bedroom (except where I had insisted on adding the window), was convenient, but Damiani had to return to the house to trim the upper doors when we discovered that they would open only halfway before hitting the sloping ceiling. These cupboards alone, made of unpainted plywood, cost over $2,000.00.

Because of the phone company's reputation for long delays in getting a phone installed, April was none too early to order the telephone ahead of the move-in date. This was a major undertaking in Italy and involved several visits to the company "Sip," a monopoly, and in my case a 45-minute drive away in Montepulciano. At headquarters I had heard that the computers were invariably down, and plenty of *lire* were charged for initiating service. Still, I knew of some instances where installation took years instead of months, so I was already ahead, having been told that I would be connected by the end of summer.

The middle-aged, pleasant but sober-looking woman who waited on Ciro and me at Sip knew who we were and smilingly told us that she was Geometra Landi's daughter! I ordered two phones and picked out the models, then requested a *contascatti*, a tabletop meter that would keep track of how much outgoing calls cost by ticking off the *scatti*, just as an odometer counts the miles on a car. Each *scatto* cost about fifteen cents, but when phoning to the US, for example, the *contascatti* sounded like a slot machine making a big payoff. The rate to the US was about four dollars a minute – a price that a state monopoly could insist on.

I was given the new phones immediately and carried them home, though there was no place yet to plug them in. A postcard arrived assigning me a phone number, 26-56-64, and that served to give me false hope that the line would soon be installed. Two months later the workmen from Sip arrived in their neat van. Soon after, a truck delivered the three new poles needed to attach a cable leading up the driveway. From the third pole to the house the cable was laid underground for a distance of about fifty feet. The two phones (minus the *contascatti*) went into operation in early August. The cost of the installation, paid well in advance: $1,200.00.

Many months later I phoned Sip to reorder the *contascatti* that had never been delivered. "Well," said the Sip employee, "the computer is down, but I can take your order by hand. I must tell you, though, that it will take six to eight months before we can install your *contascatti*; there simply aren't enough to go around" – not very encouraging, but I put in the order. The next day I got a call: "This is the phone company," said a male voice. "I'm coming out to install your *contascatti*; will you be home?" In ten minutes he had arrived and in another ten the meter was working. I didn't ask questions.

Soon after, Sip added the options that the US had offered years before: call waiting, conference calls, automatic redial, even dial-a-prayer, dial-a-recipe, and dial-a-horoscope. There were emergency numbers for battered children, drug addicts, or for information about AIDS. But the basic phone service, that of putting the caller in contact with another person via telephone, was totally unreliable. A busy signal could mean that the line was occupied, or it may have indicated that the number was no longer in service or that the phone was out of order. I was told that 49 percent of the phone calls placed over Sip did not go through properly or did not get connected at all.

One afternoon I wanted to make a local call. I pressed the number, 26-53-29. The fire department answered. "Who are you trying to call, Signora?" the fireman asked when I said that I had the wrong number. I told him the number I had called. "You dialed the fire department, 115," he said. "I didn't dial 115," I defended, "the phone dialed it by itself!"

A large percentage of the calls that did go through ended up being cut off in mid-conversation. "*E' caduta la linea.*" (literally, "the line has fallen") was a phrase heard commonly, even on the many call-in radio and TV shows.

Then cellular phones, *telefonini*, were introduced and became a status symbol. There were so many of these phones used by people while driving that a law was passed, (but not enforced) prohibiting their use while driving. After all, how could a gesticulating Italian talk and steer at the same time! The son of a friend of mine was driving, his mother in the passenger's seat. The young man was describing the previous evening's party, gesticulating as required. "Keep your hands on the wheel!" his mother ordered. "Well, then I can't tell you the story," he pouted, and silence prevailed.

5. MAY DAY AND MARKETS

May first no one was on the job. May Day was celebrated here as Labor Day is in the States. While the Communists were certainly willing to take off work on any available saint's feast day, *Primo Maggio* was the worker's special holiday, dedicated to Saint Joseph, the artisan craftsman and father of Jesus. If a flat-chested woman passed by workmen, they would say of her, "Saint Joseph's been there with his jack plane," referring to the carpenter's tool that shaves down wood. Aurelio said, "When I die I want a red rose placed on my grave every *Primo Maggio*." May first was too soon for roses to be in bloom, but there were smiling pansies and delicate iris in the moist gardens.

Most of the men in town had a dream of visiting Russia; many accomplished this goal by taking a ten-day tour that used up their savings. With the fall of Communist regimes all over Eastern Europe, the local Party members did not renew their memberships, clinging instead to the traditional ideals of the Party and declaring that Russia in particular would not survive without Communism.

There were privately owned grocery stores, or *alimentari*, but most successful was the one run by its members and even named Coop for *cooperativo*. The Coop had a one-time membership fee of ten dollars; in return it offered special buys, calendars for the New Year, gifts or generous deductions on items ranging from electric blankets to jewelry, and a savings plan that paid a higher interest rate than the local banks.

A weekly event for centuries, the *mercato* drew out all the locals. The women dressed up to do their open-air shopping. They wore high heels, usually black and worn, and sweaters with sequins and jet beads. "All dressed up and nowhere to go," Ciro derided. But the nude faces and ruined hands of these women reflected the amount of work they did. Being Communists, they rarely attended church, so their one fun outing of the week was the *mercato*.

Especially when the weather was nice everyone came to meet friends, catch up on gossip, and generally hang around in Sunday best watching one another. As the retired men met they called out good-naturedly to one another "*Stronzo!*" (turd) or "*Cornuto!*" (cuckold). Then they stood in small groups talking about crops and hunting since in public they didn't discuss women.

Meanwhile the women were busy pulling out wads of *lire* from which they extracted just enough to pay for a taffeta ribbon, a cotton undershirt, or a potted schefflera. The vendors' vans lined the street up into the main piazza with some stragglers stationed over by the park. The merchandise was displayed on trestle tables under the vendor's awning, and items on special sale were in an upside-down umbrella with a sign offering two items for one: "*Sconti, due per uno*". Hardware vendor here, bolts of cloth there, shoes, underwear (some X-rated that shocked no one), outerwear, music cassettes, sewing notions, fresh produce, live chickens and ducks, household and kitchen items, and flowers and plants were all sold by vendors assigned to one of Sarteano's allotted spaces. One

46

salesman even had beauty products including Grecian Formula and Dial soap.

There were usually two vans selling *porchetta*, roast pork, with the unfortunate porker's head on display. The fragrance of rosemary tempted the noses of those not impressed visually. Most purchasers ordered some *crostaio*, a bit of crackling skin, to go with the pork, and the vendor always added the concoction of spices including the rosemary and plenty of garlic and salt used in roasting the meat. It was absolutely scrumptious!

The mercato was a year-round event but with fewer vendors in winter. In summer there were even a couple of "*vu cumprà*" salesmen: Africans who would spread out a blanket to set up shop and unabashedly offer imitation Gucci bags, fake Lacoste shirts, and a few homemade artifacts the men had made while waiting for paying customers.

To buy fresh produce in summer at the *mercato* always meant waiting in line because of the tourists. Once during an especially hot and hectic period, another local woman and I had been waiting patiently our turn to buy some plums and apricots. Being quiet and patient had not paid off, though, as we were both upstaged by loud Roman housewives who insisted on being waited on first. Finally the other woman's endurance gave out, but rather than complain, she said good-naturedly to the vendor, "This *signora* and I were little girls here together!" The vendor smiled and paid attention to both of us.

It was general knowledge that one had to haggle with the vendors: the asked price was never paid, except for weighed produce. I had watched Ciro haggle vaguely, but I always felt he got gypped anyway. My first solo outing at the mercato I found an ivory silk camisole I wanted to buy. The price was about twenty dollars. When I asked the tired vendor what the final price was, he barked at me that there did not exist first, second, or *ultimi prezzi*, and that if I didn't like the price, don't buy the item. "I won't!" I said, dropping the blouse as if it were a rotten fish. So much for my ability to haggle.

Later I learned from watching the locals that only as they had money in hand did they ask for a small discount. Having the money visible showed the merchant that the buyer was serious, so the seller could relent knowing that the sale was made. The era of drastic discounts was history, though tourists often made fools of themselves trying anyway. Later I tried bargaining again, this time for a pack of three tee shirts. "Will you give me a discount?" I asked as I displayed a few bills. "Sure, I'll buy you a cup of coffee," meaning a markdown of a couple of thousand lire -- the price of an espresso.

To finish the shopping spree at the *mercato*, shoppers moved on to the Coop before it closed at 1:30 for lunch. These larger cooperative grocery stores had their drawbacks – such as a lack in quality, especially in fresh produce, and in the minimal personnel available to wait on customers. Lines formed to buy produce, then again for bread and deli items, and a third line at the meat counter, not to mention waiting at check-out where all items were added up on an old-fashioned cash register. While the stores were small in comparison to supermarkets in other areas, shopping took patience because of the inevitable waits on line. I would find myself behind a local housewife while she ordered kilos of apples ("not those floury ones"), salad fixings, eggplant, blood oranges, garlic, and potatoes. Finally having moved on, I could order my one bunch of grapes only to find the same woman ahead of me on the next line, where she asked for Russian salad, cheeses, fillets of anchovy, and a kilo of bread. As an afterthought she joked, "Oh, Mari', give me some of that onion pizza; I'm not kissing anyone tonight!"

Driving into Sarteano for me was like driving into my past, like reentering any small town in the States in

48

the late '50's. In late 1980's Sarteano, teenagers cruised up and down the main square on motor scooters looking for some kind of harmless diversion. Girls, all dressed alike in jeans and loose shirts, formed groups of four or five and put themselves on display on two benches, pretending not to notice the boys passing by. Parked cars were left unlocked and with the keys in the ignition. Homosexuality was still in the closet, AIDS didn't exit, and no hookers were on view, as by day they were housewives. By 10:30 at night shutters closed and the streets became deserted except during holidays. The police were not even on duty at night, and during the day often there was no one in the station to answer the phone. Racial unrest didn't exist as there were no minorities, thus no discrimination. No one went hungry (the nuns saw to that); there were no street people, no beggars.

In Sarteano, there was no cinema nor discotheque, no aerobics classes; the tiny library, open only four hours per week, went unpatronized. There were, though, at least seven hairdressers (women only, both clients and operators). The local women emerged from them feeling good about their unimaginative fuzzy permanents and coarse dye jobs, and they carried home with them hair care products under the exotic name "Afford". The women were doing their best with what was offered locally.

Outside the old walls of town, away from the main square and the main street or *corso*, were the banks, post office, and shops and apartment houses built since World War II. Most of the townspeople preferred the comfort and convenience of the more modern accommodations, but they continued to respect and love the old structures. The *centro storico* came into view just on the edge of town, including a neatly kept park and the Church of San Francesco dating from the fourteenth century. The interior walls of the church had been left free of stucco up from the floor for about three feet, partly out of historical interest, but mostly to help minimize the ever-present problem of humidity shared by all the old stone structures. Some medieval frescoes on display at San Francesco had been saved and transferred from another local church that had been bombed during the war, but the most important art treasure, an oil "Annunciation" by Beccafumi of the Sienese School, was housed in another church, San Martino, near the highest point in town.

The *centro storico* featured private apartments with heavy wooden doors on the stone facades and the indispensable balcony above. Some facades still had the centuries-old wrought iron rings to secure horses' reins and the second story torch holders from medieval times. Unlike in those days, however, the gutters did not pour water directly into the street. Instead, in modern times each downspout disappeared into the wall of these apartment buildings and connected with the sewer system below.

Along with the stores and apartments on the *corso* was one of the certainties of modern life: a bar. But not what Americans think of as a bar; it was more a refreshment bar offering cool drinks and snacks, not so much a place to buy alcohol. A prerequisite of an Italian bar is that it have a few tables outdoors, no matter the environment. The tables may be under a tree or on the curb of a busy road. At this particular bar some local elderly men passed the afternoon playing cards, and in the evening the bar was the hangout for young people. One of the regulars in the afternoon was the local veterinarian, an older man with a huge nose. I overheard a stranger in town asking the pretty blue-eyed owner of the bar where he could find the vet. She replied with typical Tuscan humor: "He's right outside playing cards;" she smiled, "the one without a nose."

Sarteano did have a few drunks, some of whom wandered the streets, blabbering to passersby. One particularly colorful man, a native Sarteanan and a sculptor, was always on tour around the *centro storico*. Usually under the influence, he dressed with care everyday in his multicolored outfits with matching accessories. He had the extraordinary given name of Plinio. While I knew of the ancient Roman authors Pliny the Elder and his son Pliny the Younger, I suspected that this local man was not named for them directly. The Sarteano Pliny, Plinio, walked the town for the purpose of accepting admiration along the way. When I met him (on the street, of course), he cheerfully and unabashedly told me what a talented and successful sculptor he was, and he said that he would give me his autograph "with a nice dedication." This attitude, proud or even pretentious, was common and considered appropriate, coming from him and from many others. How else would people know how great you are if you yourself didn't tell them! Sarteano had great pride in its citizens and their accomplishments. Monetary wealth was not the most important indication of success.

Alcoholism was considered a family problem and was kept as quiet as possible. Drugs, however, were beginning to invade the town on a larger scale. I had seen some glassy-eyed young people and had heard gossip about a supplier or two. There was even talk about a foreign couple, residents of many years, who "went often to South America." Two drug-related scandals could not easily be hushed up. A son of one of the first families of Sarteano died from an overdose, and gossip was fast and furious for several weeks with all the details. Then a group of twelve teenagers, most from good, hardworking families, were arrested for theft (their loot was found in a farmhouse near mine) and drug possession. This news really hit the townspeople hard, with an attitude of "it could have been my kid." Drugs had come to stay.

From my house I could see on nearby Monte Cetona a restored Franciscan monastery. It was founded in 1212 by Saint Francis, who often stopped there on his way to Rome. Then it became the project of a brother of that order who took over the facility in the 1970s and made it into a rehabilitation center for recovering drug addicts, renaming it Mondo X. The young people were from all walks of life and many European countries. Anyone was considered eligible to enter the program, no matter his economic, religious, or patriotic background.

Referred to as "*Padre*", the brother in charge was not a typical Franciscan. He was said to wear cashmere sports jackets and sunglasses and to have his own helicopter pad at the monastery. But as one of the residents of the center told me, shaking her head: "They say a lot of things about the *padre*." The income to run the center came from private sources, not the Church. The recovering addicts worked hard at farming, gardening, and restoring and maintaining the buildings and grounds they occupied. They ran an exclusive restaurant and gift shop selling homemade crafts: olive wood sculptures, needlework, and jams. Whether or not the Franciscan was atypical of his brother monks, he had been successful in helping these young addicts build new and healthy lives for themselves. I wondered how they could survive the real world after having lived in the oasis they themselves had created. Certain of the young people were assigned to give the guided tours, often in several languages, with the most timid residents having been given this duty so as to overcome their shyness.

6. *"TU"* OR *"LEI"*?

On the street in town Ciro and I kept running into the same crook I had seen in the Office of Statistics the first week in Sarteano. He was the one who had teased Felice, the gruff man who had waited on me. The leather jacket, slim mustache, and sneaky eyes convinced me that this man about town was a shady character. Astonishingly, he turned out to be Gianmarco, Sarteano's police chief, innocently patrolling the streets as part of his job.

Soon Gianmarco began coming around to the house after the *operaii* had gone home. He said that he wanted to know if we needed anything and asked how the work was going. By the third time we saw him, he gave me the *tu*, the intimate pronoun for "you," an affront that aggravated Ciro considerably. Not to be beneath Gianmarco, I gave him the *tu* in return. Soon after, he began propositioning me when we were out of Ciro's earshot. Clearly he was married as he wore a thick gold wedding band. He asked me, "Are you really married to that man?" When I told him, "Of course!" he mumbled, *"Che peccato . . ."* Being married to Ciro may have had its negatives, but I didn't consider it what

Gianmarco referred to as "a shame." Gianmarco, of course, was thinking of my sex life.

We never progressed beyond the propositioning stage, though that continued for months - no, years! - yet he was never more aggressive than to take my hand. An American living nearby, a woman younger and prettier than I, compared notes with me as to Gianmarco's come on. We found that his strategy and sweet talk text did not vary at all. It differed, though, from an American man's flirtation in its honesty. He would say the usual – ". . . love you . . . , beautiful . . . , hold you . . . ," blah, blah blah. Then, candidly, he would add, "Of course, I can't see you on Sunday or my days off because I spend that time with my wife and family."

Gianmarco was the only new acquaintance who gave me the *tu*. English-speaking people, for the most part unknowingly, use these intimate pronouns all the time (except for at least some religious sects that I know of). Otherwise, using the formal pronoun we would sound as if we were quoting Shakespeare or the King James version of the Bible: "Would thou care to dine with me?" "I love thee. . ."

An analogy with the English language use of these intimate pronouns is being on a first-name basis with a person. Even that, though, is not equal to the *tu* since, in America at least, surnames are almost neglected and first names used immediately.

Since the Second World War and with the growth of communism, Italians use the *tu* more frequently and easily. They are not like the French, who in some instances don't even give the *tu* to their spouses. Italian children being using the formal *Lei* at about age seven when they enter grade school. Before that, they give the *tu* to everyone. Children are given the *tu* until they reach their early twenties and show themselves to be adults.

54

If it were up to me, I would use the *tu* and forget the *Lei*, in the first place to avoid the inevitable class discrimination. I refuse to abide by the old class distinction rule, that of the upper class giving the *tu* to all beneath them socially while the lower class use only the *Lei* to address their so-called superiors. I know an American woman who married a Tuscan nobleman and from that moment felt free to use the *tu* with everyone. Her husband was mortified when she gave the *tu* to the local priest.

There is a sublime moment when one passes from the *Lei* to the *tu*. Clearly it brings an intimacy to a relationship which needs no further definition, whether between two of the same or opposite sex. When Gattone suggested that he and I start using the *tu*, I had to tell him that it was inappropriate. It would have been unprofessional. Ours was strictly a job-related relationship; the *Lei* remained between us.

Many times Italians use the *tu* in private but the *Lei* in public. Socially I give the *tu* to my physician, but in his office I revert to the formal. This can get confusing to the people involved, who end up using both pronouns in the same conversation. Sometimes a man gives the *tu* to a woman, usually while coming on to her, until his wife appears, when he quickly takes on a serious expression and calls the woman "Signora."

But these pronouns play only a small part in learning how the Italian language is used. The people of Sarteano are proud of being Tuscan, but being on the border with Umbria they don't speak pure, clear Italian as Dante intended. Syllables are dropped, accents switched to another syllable, the sex of nouns altered. Once the dialect is deciphered, conversation is easy because the verb endings are often nonexistent. *Vado* becomes *v'o*, *facciamo* is *f'amo*, and *mangiare* turned into *mania'*. These speech patterns change only a few kilometers away. To the west in Val d'Orcia is one dialect; to the east across the border into Umbria is another.

No word can end in a consonant; it seems that the Tuscan tongue cannot help but wangle a vowel onto every word. "Ann" has to be "Anna." When I cried "Ouch," Aurelio would laugh and say, "Ouchy" without realizing he had added the vowel. The small truck called a pickup in America had its name transformed into "P-Kappa" in Italy. My dog Puff got rechristened Puffi, which I actually preferred.

Many common phrases are literally sung, especially when a disagreement is going on. To put emphasis on "You can't do that!" they sing, "*Non si può*," dividing "*può-ò*'" into two notes. *Recitativo* is alive and well in the streets of today's Tuscany, not to be heard only in opera houses.

Aside from Gattone and the *operai*, one early attempt in deciphering the dialect came from my neighbor Manlio. He drove his tractor up to the front of Il Poggetto and killed the noisy diesel engine but did not dismount his iron horse. He had come to introduce himself, which I appreciated. He did not linger. It was lunchtime and he said he was going home to eat: "*Allora, Signora, v'o a manià. Buondì,*" he saluted as he started the engine and left towards home.

Manlio and his family were a good example of how Sarteano was changing. He was one of the last sharecroppers, a *mezzadro* who farmed for an absentee landlord, who in turn received half of Manlio's yield: *mezzo* means "half". Manlio was provided a house and several hectares of land to cultivate. He had a few cows, hogs, and chickens, and he, his wife, and their three grown children lived upstairs and the animals downstairs as it had been originally at Il Poggetto. His work was endless, and at about fifty years of age Manlio looked and moved like an old man.

His family all wanted Manlio to take early retirement so they could move into town. As it was, the children didn't help with the chores, and they wanted to get away from the grip of the absentee landlord. The farmhouse had no central heat, and they lived with the constant stink and noise of the animals below. Anything in town would be better than their present condition, they rationalized. The three children wanted to get married, to have families of their own. Moving into town would be a way to improve their social standing and make it easier to have friends. In the end Manlio consented, and once in town he couldn't believe his good fortune. Life was easy at last!

7. UNEXPECTED LOVE

At last in June, two months after my arrival in Sarteano, the weather began improving. Wild flowers were blooming, and the racy red poppies, delicate lavender sweet peas, and happy daisies filled my fields. Fragrant Scotch broom skirted the road to the house. The real-life cuckoos sang 31 o'clock, and a nightingale had made its home in the tiny woods adjacent my property. The swallows had returned from Africa, and one pair chattered as they built a nest in my carport.

Aurelio sang with more fervor: "*Quanto sarebbe bello far' l'amor' con te*," he improvised, dreaming of "how beautiful it would be to make love to you". I asked him to make a *beretto* for me, the brown paper hat like he wore; then I stuck some yellow broom flowers in the brim "to be feminine," I explained. I was beginning to feel at home, in a place I could live in contentedly. As my Italian improved I could enjoy the local humor and appreciate the importance of individual dignity. The beauty of my surroundings was incomparable.

Puff, now Puffi, had adopted Il Poggetto. She began growling at unknown intruders when they came up the driveway. When she barked for the first time, after weeks of silence, the *operai* applauded. "I didn't think she knew how," joked Nino. Ciro still wouldn't let me go to the house alone; he always came along, allowing a superficial view of the work being done before he whisked me away to go to town or to rehearse. He cautioned me to be wary not only of strangers, but of my workers. "Don't ever get into a car with one of them," he warned. "These Italians always try to take advantage of foreign girls." I couldn't imagine such a thing from any of my *operai*, but I kept my distance. I remembered all times in Florida when returning home after running errands, Ciro would be waiting for me in the driveway, ready to chastise me for my tardiness but relieved to see me. There his fears were general: an accident, the car breaking down, a delay in traffic. Now he worried that an Italian man would force his attentions on me. As for me, the last thing I had in mind was a flirtation of any kind.

One morning arriving at the house as usual, Aurelio took me by the arm, up the stairs, and pointed from a window that still had no glass. At the edge of the *oliveto* he had planted several rows of flowers for me. In front of us on a windowsill was a flowerpot with lavender petunias and a pink impatiens growing in it. His sweet thoughtfulness really got to me, and I began looking at him as an individual, not just one of the *operai*. He began calling me "Signora Susi," looking me straight in the eye and grinning as he said it.

Suddenly a few days later Aurelio told me he wouldn't be back to work at Il Poggetto, that Gattone had assigned him to another job. I was desperate. I had come to rely on Aurelio for everything to do with the house. He had made himself indispensable; I needed him if I intended to go ahead with my property's improvement. I had to decide whether I would limp along doing things halfway and super-economically as Ciro and Raffaella wanted, or whether I was going to continue to involve

60

this knowledgeable artisan. I went to Gattone's home in town, but no one was there. I left a note on the door pleading with Gattone not to take away Aurelio, my *braccio destro* (right arm). When Gattone came to Il Poggetto the next day, I begged with tears in my eyes. Gattone said simply, "Aurelio's not going anywhere." The threat to leave had been staged by Aurelio to get my reaction. I was so relieved that I didn't care that Aurelio had tested me in this boyish way.

Aurelio brought me red roses from his garden; he returned in the evening after work to do extras like hang light fixtures. Once, taking a folded yardstick from me, he ran his hand down my bare arm. Ciro said, "He's either a saint or a nut, maybe both, and he's got a fixation on you. Watch out: he might leave his wife or even kill you, he's the type. He could create a scandal and I would be the victim!" Ciro could not even imagine what this artisan's attention might mean to me.

Not long before we had to vacate Raffaella's house so that her summer tenants could take it over, new terracotta tiles were laid in the upstairs studio at "Il Poggetto." The walls had been plastered and the windows installed. Since there was no plumbing yet, we couldn't move in, but we were able to move the pianos in once the floor tiles had set. The workmen themselves made the move using a tiny Ape.

The Ape, a three-wheeled motorcycle-powered workhorse, is named for the strong, energetic bee, not the English word for a primate. The driver needs no license, so farmers of all mental capacities find these vehicles indispensable for work and general transportation. This time, two workmen and I rode inside the intimate cab of the Ape while the pianos were tied on the rear open bed. The other four workers ran alongside. My fear was that one or both of the pianos would slide off the Ape as we made the steep turn up my driveway.

61

Moving a piano takes special skill; it is, after all, a delicate musical instrument, not just a piece of furniture. Once before in Tuscany we had rented uprights like these that had to be brought up an exterior staircase. That time it took two men, the music store proprietor and his son, both of whom were smaller than the average Italian. They moved with slow, even steps and when finished weren't even out of breath. This time it took five men, each with a different idea of how the project should be approached. Usually imperturbable, lanky Fabio couldn't cope with the job and just watched. Slowly one piano then the other was lifted up the rebuilt outdoor staircase and wheeled into the new studio. At last the piano benches were brought in with a flourish – they seemed so light after the weight of the pianos. In the end all the men were gasping and panting, and Aurelio was holding his heart. Within a few minutes each man recovered and shared our joy at seeing the pianos side-by-side in their new home, the upstairs studio overlooking the olive grove.

Ciro and I practiced on the pianos that same day. With bare walls and tiled floors, the instruments seemed amplified, their sound booming. Undaunted by the acoustics, we rehearsed separately during working hours, then went over our duo program in the evening after the workmen had gone home. Ciro took his solo turn early in the afternoon, then I had to practice. Admittedly I wanted to show off for Aurelio and Fabio, working just outside the closed studio door. They remained quiet while I ran through my pieces. I chomped at Bach, poured liquid Rachmaninoff, and sizzled through Gershwin. At the end I emerged from my practice, trying to look noncommittal but secretly anxious for their response. Knowing how these men didn't wish to interfere with my work, I couldn't expect applause, compliments, or even a nod of approval, but I was eager for some reaction. Because they didn't say anything, I commented, "I prefer your songs," which removed their shyness at not knowing what to say. I went into the master bedroom to take some measurements, and in a few minutes heard Aurelio singing, "I kneel before you . . . , I'm not worthy of you . . ."

Having the practice pianos at Il Poggetto meant we were there, on hand, much more during the day. This new set of musical circumstances, including my unsophisticated audience, was more foreign to me than any other cultural differences in comparison with the States. From the several shows on which Ciro and I collaborated, he arranged all the songs for voice and duo-pianos. For our most recent musical comedy, still a work in progress, we had a one-hour long narration with music in which we shared telling the story and singing each song, introduced with bits of dialogue. This audition became a tour de force which the two of us performed hundreds of times in various places: in our own Florida home, in society mansions from New York to Palm Beach, at the Dramatists' Guild above Sardi's in New York, and in theaters with an invited audience of potential backers. On those occasions, the women wore colorful silks and strong perfume. They applauded and cooed compliments while their tanned husbands announced that our show would be the next big hit on Broadway. Somehow no checkbooks were drawn from cashmere sport coats or Fendi purses, but we became known on the society circuit.

A few days after the pianos were moved into Il Poggetto, Aurelio was there alone, digging an enormous hole at the foot of the driveway. Unaware of my own growing interest in this man, innocently I walked down to see what he was doing. After a moment he put down his shovel. "I have to leave here, I can't stand it," he said. "Every time I look in your eyes you make me feel like a boy in love for the first time. Will you go out with me?" As he spoke I could see that he was shaking. In answering him I used the *tu* for the first time between us. "First of all," I said sternly, "I'm not that kind of woman." I saw the hurt in his eyes, so added in a softer tone, "You can't leave me, Aurelio; I need you for the house." He, using the *tu*, answered, "And I need you." I went back up to the house confused and afraid.

The next day all the workmen were downstairs breaking through the 18-inch thick wall where a door was to be added. Nino was in charge and today didn't feel like whistling. Aurelio hammered at the stubborn wall, his muscular arms covered with rock dust. The *operai* must have seen how love-struck Aurelio was, especially with such visible evidence as the patch of flowers he had planted. Nino said to me in front of the others, "Watch out for Aurelio; he has a lot of women." I tried not to react but was desolate at the idea that Aurelio had been after me merely as an addition to his collection. With a smile I asked Nino, "I wonder why? He's not that good-looking; it must be his way with words." Nino said simply, "He's a rascal."

A few minutes later I was able to speak alone outside to Aurelio: "Now I understand everything. *Che peccato.*" Just as Gianmarco had called my being married to Ciro a shame, I now used the phrase to describe Aurelio's actions towards me. But Aurelio denied Nino's accusation: "I swear on my children it's not true!" He kicked an empty bucket and sent it flying into the front field: "The men always make me the brunt of their jokes." I wanted to believe him.

The following morning Aurelio and Fabio were working on the septic system. As usual Aurelio was doing the heavy work, and at one point was in a hole supporting the weight of the concrete tank. I said to Fabio, "Do you think after this one of his many women will give him a back rub?" Fabio caught on – "Absolutely. If not the first one, then another will be right behind her." Aurelio was hurt: "Even you tease me, Signora? Why?" We were both upset, not knowing what to do, what to believe.

Ciro had influenced me to be wary of these men, and it wasn't only out of his jealousy. *Furbo*, being clever and cunning in relationships, was a way of life I didn't know and couldn't recognize, so I worried that Aurelio wanted my attention for ulterior motives, starting with Il Poggetto itself, yet my intuition told me to trust him.

Aurelio continued bringing me homegrown flowers, then cherries and strawberries, and he kept asking me when I would go out with him. Finally I made a badly prepared speech. "I've come here to live," I said. "I want you to be my friend, but I don't want gossip in town. I can't risk a scandal. Besides, I told you, I don't fool around; I'm not that type." He was crestfallen, and in my heart I repented immediately. I went upstairs and tried to hide my tears from the other workmen around. Later that day I handed Aurelio a note: "You must understand that I am afraid. I don't dare. It isn't that I don't want to." He gave me a tender, loving look and without a word handed me back the note.

The next day was rainy. Work went on as usual. Ciro practiced the piano while I watched the men at their tasks. Aurelio stole glances at me and at one point brushed his lips across my cheek as he took my hand. After work, when all the men had gone home, as usual Ciro and I rehearsed our upcoming piano program for Chartres, then for once Ciro wanted to practice again on his own. I stood outside under the scaffolding against the front of the house. There were still a couple of hours of daylight left, but the weather was drizzly and unfriendly, and I felt lonely. Then Aurelio arrived, driving up the road at 50 miles an hour and honking the horn. Ciro heard nothing because of his loud piano playing in the acoustically live room upstairs.

Aurelio, cleaned up and wearing a plaid shirt, jumped out of the car, ran over, and grabbing my hand began pulling me into the downstairs. The door was barred from the inside, but before I had time to say no, he had climbed through an open window, opened the door, and now was pulling me through it. He held me so tightly I could barely breathe. It seemed he could reach clear around me with one arm. With his first kiss I thought, "Thank God for sending me this man." He said, "I love you, Susi, *ti amo*. This is forever." I remember saying, "I'm cooked."

We didn't make love. I was too nervous and afraid, and Aurelio wasn't pushing me. Besides, outside it was raining, and in the yet to be renovated downstairs, there was nothing but a dirt floor. But it didn't matter. Aurelio made me feel secure and happier than I had felt in a long, long time.

8. *APPARTAMENTO* IN TOWN

Il Poggetto predictably was not ready for occupancy, not even the second story, by the tenth of June as promised. Raffaella's high-paying summer tenants would arrive in a few days, so where were we to go? All the hotels and *pensioni* were full, and with Puffi we were three. Boxes of household items were arriving daily from the States and needed to be stored somewhere dry. Gattone double-talked double-time, but at the last minute he arranged for us to have a tiny apartment in town, gratis, for the month of June.

I went to Gattone's house to pick up the keys to the apartment. Intentionally I arrived at an hour when Gattone would not be home. His wife, whose name Gattone had failed to mention, greeted me with forced enthusiasm. She was a plump, dyed blonde who tried very hard to be what she considered feminine, speaking in a baby voice and wearing a frilly blouse and bright lipstick. She teetered in the kind of high heels most local women didn't even own. She wanted to befriend me, as I was a *signora* and she a social climber in a town that offered no place to climb. When I politely refused her offer of coffee, she took offense. I couldn't come to her

67

house and not accept some refreshment. Even though it was only 10 in the morning, she gave me a Cointreau. As soon as I could take my leave, I reeled out of the house, apartment keys in hand. At least now we had a place to live temporarily.

The new accommodations were in a building that had six apartments on two stories. Ours was in the back of the second floor, overlooking the owners' vegetable garden. We had a tiny entrance terrace strung with a clothesline entwined in a grapevine. The entry led directly into the closet-sized kitchen, where a large TV sat on top of the refrigerator. Then there was a bathroom with a tub and a bedroom with four beds, including bunk beds. The owners, Everardo and Bianca, lived in the adjacent apartment.

Bianca, fifty or so, was the business half of the couple. She was high-strung and a type who needed a lot of drama in life. She told us that she had dangerously high blood pressure, but whenever we saw her she was drinking coffee and smoking a cigarette. She was about forty pounds overweight, and she spent her mornings cooking, as did many of the local women. She gave us samples of her excellent dishes: the veal stew called *spezzatino*, her *ragù* or her slowly simmered minestrone, made with local vegetables. Her idea of conversation was to complain as much as possible.

Bianca's fair-haired husband complemented her. He had been the painter of the upstairs interior at Il Poggetto and had simply painted the two bathrooms with a plasticized textured paint, resolving my problem with the vinyl wallpaper. Everardo had a gentlemanly manner about him, so Ciro referred to him as *S'or* Everardo, an informal way of calling him Signor' Everardo.

I enjoyed staying in the town of Sarteano. There was a lovely, shady garden in front of the house, a relief after the mud at Il Poggetto. Walking distance to the bank, post office, and Coop were wonderful advantages. In the evening the townspeople strolled by leisurely, out for their postprandial walk, perhaps stopping in a bar for hazelnut or *gianduia* ice cream.

One evening Aurelio came by our cubbyhole. He was freshly shaved and cologned, wearing a white dress shirt, a gray jacket, pressed pants, and leather loafers – and he had no hat on this time. We were just finishing dinner. He wouldn't sit down at our small table, so I stood up. He refused a glass of wine: "I never drink outside of meals," he explained. As Ciro interviewed him about his work, I had a chance to study him. It was purely a social call, an excuse to see me. When I accompanied him out to the balcony, he shyly kissed my hand – a far cry from our passionate kiss in the damp downstairs of Il Poggetto. The next morning on the job he was all business; only the clean scent of his cologne lingered as a reminder of his visit.

One sunny afternoon while we were rehearsing yet again the Gershwin duo music at Il Poggetto, Raffaella came walking up the drive escorted by a priest. She introduced us to don Paolo, the local *parroco*, the parish priest. Don Paolo was white-haired but vigorous, of average size and shape, and on this occasion he was a little tipsy. He enthused over Raffaella, ". . .*una brava persona*," admired the view from the house, and praised the weather, the countryside, Ciro and me. He had come down from town to bless devout Raffaella's house, so she had invited him to bless my house as well. Being neither Italian nor Catholic, I had never been to a house blessing before: it sounded interesting. Ciro hung around to see what would happen. The *operai* continued plastering the walls, but kept a constant eye on don Paolo. The priest added a stole to his habit and opened his prayer book. We were standing in the unfinished upstairs living room in front of the fireplace, the workmen in the master bedroom. After reading a couple of passages of scripture, don Paolo invited us to recite the Lord's Prayer. He was intrigued to hear it in *americano*. I ended up reciting it alone in my mother tongue as Ciro didn't know it – another lapse in his education. Some holy water was sprinkled, and the ceremony ended. During the blessing don Paolo had changed face completely and was serious, but as soon as he finished the last Ave Maria he was back to his jolly enthusiasm. Ciro couldn't resist telling the priest that I had been a church organist and choir director in America. Don Paolo's eyes doubled in size: "We have a pipe organ at San Francesco. You must come and play it!"

After the house had been properly sanctified, don Paolo accompanied Raffaella back down the driveway. The *operai* were relieved to see them go. The priest had greeted some of them by name, embarrassing them: they were strong Communists and wanted to disassociate themselves from anything to do with the Church. Aurelio, who hadn't been inside a church since his marriage twenty-five years earlier, picked up a paintbrush he was using to wet down a wall. "Here's how to bless a house," he mumbled as he sprinkled the wall using the same gesture as don Paolo with the holy water.

While the first water to arrive at Il Poggetto may have been holy, procuring running water for the house was one of the biggest problems to be solved. Raffaella had a hookup with the town water, but at City Hall they wanted me to pay for the installation of the larger pipes that would be necessary if I were to join the line. Already my sharecropper neighbor Manlio complained that his farm got no water when Raffaella turned hers on full force, pulling all the pressure down to her house. The new pipes would have to come from the main road a kilometer away and would cost $3,000, a sum both Ciro and I considered prohibitive.

70

The obvious solution was to dig a well. There was an abundance of water everywhere around Il Poggetto. The winery next door was by a stream, Raffaella had two wells, and another neighbor, Burani, had veins gushing in various parts of his property.

Word circulated among the *operai* that we needed a diviner. The first one to come around was Michele, our heavy equipment subcontractor. He said, "Here only ten meters from the house there is a vein. Dig five or six meters down and you'll hit water. No *problema*." Just for the fun of it, four or five other diviners came around, some using twigs, some with a sort of spinning pendulum to help them find the right spot to dig the well. One man, not a local, was found by Raffaella and Ciro who, in their impatient, slapdash manner, took the matter into their hands. Their usual "we have to hurry" mantra took them to the Yellow Pages: "It must be a reliable company if they are in the Pagine Gialle," Raffaella concluded. I wanted to wait the extra few days to hire someone I knew was reputable, but Raffaella and Ciro prevailed yet again.

Representing the company found in the Yellow Pages was a pasty, shifty-eyed laborer who, on his arrival, simply broke a nondescript twig off a bush and claimed to divine with it. Against my better judgment the man was hired. His estimate for the well was a depth of fifteen meters in a different location from Michele's spot and nowhere near where the others had indicated water. There was no contract with the man, just the often-used handshake between him and Ciro. Ciro, feeling *furbo*, told me that there was nothing to lose, as without a contract the handshake carried no weight: the guy couldn't make us pay if no water was found.

On June 5 the sleazy-looking man and his two cadaverous assistants arrived with an enormous number of rusty pipes and equipment with which to send the pipes toward the center of the earth. Naturally no work

71

was done that first day; it was enough to unload the pipes and lay them out. The second day it rained; the third day they began digging. At fifteen meters, the estimated depth to find water, the man said, "We hit a trickle, but it's not enough to merit a well; it would yield only about fifty liters a day." Fifty liters sounded like a lot of water to me, but the digging continued.

The fourth day Ciro had arranged for us to make an overnight getaway to Rome to visit old friends, an attorney and his wife. Ciro was fed up with Il Poggetto and its endless problems and felt he was not getting enough attention. Raffaella stayed behind to supervise the digging. When we returned two days later, Aurelio greeted me with "*Ben tornata, Signora,*" but rather than "welcome back," what he really meant was, "Wait till you see the mess that has been made in your absence." There was a dry hole 63 meters deep, plus a new hole on my neighbor Burani's property fifteen meters deep, also dry.

"When I saw that they were getting nowhere," explained Raffaella, "I decided to plea your case with Burani. He has endless water and had shown me a spot near your property line where he was sure there was a vein. He said that the water was down about five meters. Even though it was on his property, he was willing to let you put the well there. But he was wrong as they didn't find water."

I was naïve, shy, intimidated, and foreign, but even I knew better than to dig a well on someone else's property. Raffaella had her own way of rationalizing everything and felt exonerated in the whole episode. As for me, I was grateful that water had not been found on Burani's property, as I knew the well would have ended up in his name.

But this was not the end. Ciro was wrong about not having to pay the diggers if they didn't strike water. After consulting the attorney friend in Rome, I had to face facts: I was left no alternative but to write a check for $2,200.00 for two holes that were quietly filled in by my workmen. I ended up getting town water without having to pay for new pipes simply because Raffaella made such a nuisance of herself at City Hall. The water commissioner finally gave his permission at Raffaella's insistence, but he warned that the existing pipes were too small to carry enough water to supply both our houses plus Manlio's farm up the road. In fact, I ended up with part-time water. If Raffaella had hers running to do laundry or water the garden, I was left without, and my pipes filled up with air. Then when the water finally did return to me, it was combined with so much air, the faucets burped and spurted water for several feet in every direction.

Phoning the water commissioner's office became a daily task. I felt that I had a right to the water and that the town was responsible to resolve the problem of its going downhill to Raffaella's house rather than coming uphill to mine. Finally one morning, after various phone calls, I found the road to success. "*Si?*" answered a sleepy voice at the water commissioner's office. "*Buon giorno*, this is the signora at Il Poggetto. There is no water again this morning," I said. "*Si, Signora*," the voice yawned. "Not even enough to make coffee!" I exclaimed. The man at the other end of the line woke up: "Well, everyone has a right to coffee! I'll send a workman down to see what's wrong," he promised. And he did, but without larger pipes nothing could be done, I was told yet again.

The only way for me to resolve the problem was to install a cistern that automatically filled up when water was plentiful, thus ensuring a constant supply of this precious resource. I had learned through this expensive and inconvenient lesson that yet another Tuscan saying is true: you are more likely to be offered a glass of wine in Tuscany than a glass of water.

Just before leaving for the two days in Rome, I had asked Aurelio to do a special job for me. It occurred to me that at the end of my bathtub I needed some shelves and fortunately, space was available. Aurelio was working on the installation of the bathroom fixtures, his arms covered with dirt, when I called to him: "Aurelio?" "*Comandi!*" he responded, standing up from his work to face me. I suggested the plan to him, and we discussed the project at length. The shelves were to be about six inches deep by twenty long, each equidistant above the other, made of brick and plaster. Aurelio took on the job with fervor. All day he worked to please me, perfecting every measurement. Ordinarily he would have had them done in an hour, but I had asked him especially, and he relished working on them as a favor to me. He said, "I have nothing to offer you but the work I can do with my hands."

9. MOVING DAY

Towards the end of June we were finally preparing to move into the upstairs of the house, the downstairs remaining only gutted. After a couple of trips to the electric company, I was given permission to continue using the line that had been installed temporarily for the contractor. The new plumbing fixtures worked, but we had no hot water yet. We bought a small gas burner, the kind campers use, to cook on and put it in the fireplace Nino had built.

Damiani hadn't delivered the cupboard-style closets yet, so I put a metal rod across two sawhorses for hanging our clothes. In a secondhand furniture shop, we found some 1950s vintage bedroom furniture and bought new bed frames and mattresses. With the addition of a homemade table to eat on and a few straight chairs, we had enough furniture to get us by.

June 26 was moving day. Ciro stayed at Il Poggetto while I went back to the apartment in town to finish packing. Instead of pants, I wore a pale green sundress to reflect the excitement of moving day. Aurelio had arranged to borrow an Ape for the afternoon to transfer the boxes and our other belongings from town down to the house. He loaded everything, and leaving the rambling rose bushes and artichoke fronds of our landlords' garden we headed for Il Poggetto. But Aurelio and I had something in mind besides moving boxes, and as we drove through town shoulder to shoulder in the Ape cab, I felt that everyone was glaring at us, passing moral judgment on our thoughts.

Aurelio pulled off the main road into an *oliveto*. The ground had been newly mowed and was dry. He spread a blanket under an olive tree and we made tender, sweet love. Being in the open, clean air I felt far from Il Poggetto and Ciro and began to relax. My shortcomings in the language made no difference to Aurelio or me. We didn't need to talk. We weren't shy or embarrassed. For a brief time we were under no pressure and simply saw and felt and tasted each other intensely but tenderly, *pian piano*. Afterwards I knew nothing would be the same for either of us.

I had never been unfaithful to my husband, despite the fact that there was no longer a physical relationship between us. Now I felt that I had been alone for so long, with no one to care for me, to love me, and here I was convinced that I had found in Aurelio someone who was sincere in his advances, and I didn't want to say no anymore. I was still afraid, but not of Aurelio. It was no longer a case of the American not understanding the culture of the newly adopted country, nor of the Latin lover with his conquest; it was simply Aurelio and me.

When we finally arrived at about 5:30 at Il Poggetto, Ciro came rushing out: "Where have you been?" he shouted. I was petrified. "The Signora had to wait for me," Aurelio rescued immediately. "I had to get the Ape, then load it." "Oh," said Ciro, mollified. That was the first of our many excuses, intrigues, cover-ups, and lies. Aurelio said that I became a *professoressa* at finding ways of appeasing Ciro's suspicions, and it was true. I was willing to risk anything for my relationship with Aurelio. He had brought me back to life.

I remembered my early months with Ciro, when I first lived with him and the years before we finally married. He had always been a playboy, persuading any female he could charm into his arms. I thought, naively, that he would change when I moved in with him. Instead he would phone and invite a woman to lunch at our apartment, whether I were there or not. Then thinking I was out of earshot, the other woman (or was I the other woman?) inevitably asked, "But what about Susan?" Ciro tossed off, "Oh, she's just here . . . " Despite this sort of humiliation, I stayed with him.

After spending the first night at Il Poggetto, I was up early the next morning, as the workmen arrived at 7:30 everyday. All the men were on the job – except Aurelio. He was nowhere to be found, and his car wasn't parked in its usual spot under a shady oak tree. I thought, "Oh no, he's not even at work this morning. He's gloating over his conquest, and all the *operai* know that he made love to me yesterday." It was no better than one of Ciro's casual encounters. I had blatantly betrayed the morals taught me only to find myself made a fool of, "another conquest," "another notch in the belt." I had sunk into the slime category. Just then, there he was. "How well you look today, Signora," he said with a dear, secret look between us. He had been working down in front of the house where I couldn't see him; his car was being repaired in town. From that first day he never gave me any reason to doubt his love or faithfulness to me.

I hadn't been very well for a couple of years. Inexplicably I had lost twelve pounds, then another five after arriving in Sarteano. My formerly voluptuous figure, with its eye appeal, had become shapeless. Whenever I was quietly upset, which was often, Aurelio would say, "Don't worry about anything. Try to eat; you're losing too much weight. If you don't gain some back you'll never see the dust of August." The emotional and physical strain of sixteen years with Ciro had finally caught up with me.

For many years, I had had to practice the piano on my own as well as with Ciro, take care of our correspondence and pay bills, arrange the house and do kitchen duty. Most of all I was on call 24 hours a day. Ciro yelled for me constantly, so much so that it had become a joke among our friends back in the US: "Su-u-u-san, where are my glasses?" he would ask, and he would interrupt whatever I might be doing. His energy, stamina, and drive were greater than mine, even though I was so much younger than he, and I had little opportunity to rest or just have time to myself.

Now I cried a lot, but it was not always out of unhappiness. Often I cried out of relief or pleasure. Sometimes Aurelio would keep me company, and we would cry in each other's arms, then end up laughing. I was in the midst of a mid-life crisis.

One afternoon Ciro and I were in the future kitchen when he lit into me with one of his ferocious tongue-lashings. The *operai*, including Aurelio, were in the adjacent former pigsty, remodeling it into a bathroom. I had accepted Michele's bill for his hours of work operating the road grader and backhoe and had paid him immediately. I didn't want to get the same reputation that Raffaella already had of dragging her feet for months before paying her debts and always negotiating a lower price. But Ciro yelled at me, "You must never pay a bill without discussing it with the workman. He took you as a stupid, rich American who doesn't care what she spends, always smiling, throwing her money around."

I was mortified in front of the men. Afterwards when Ciro had stormed out, Aurelio came to me with tears in his eyes. "You don't deserve that. You're too sweet . . . He's much older than you; you'll have a life

78

after him, and I'll find you wherever you are. I'll take you far away," he whispered. " Il Poggetto is mine, not his," I said, "and I want to live here. I've already come from faraway." Aurelio promised, "I'll always be here with you, you're too important to me."

Aurelio began taking me to his favorite places, all of which were outdoors, in the hills above Sarteano. If it were evening, he would find the last patch of sun to stretch out under.

Now the dry season, the summer heat would not abate until late August when thundershowers broke. If the day were too hot to be comfortable, we would walk in the refreshing pine woods. Rarely did we see another person. Often we made love with the sounds and smells of the woods to help soothe our nerves. Aurelio began teaching me the various calls of the birds -- the blackbird, the magpie. He showed me how to recognize where the wild hare had passed silently and the imprint of a wild boar. Some of the plants he pointed out were traditional cures for headache or toothache. Once I reached to pick a wildflower when he shouted, "Don't touch that!" Its leaves hid stems full of sticklers. "That's the mother-in-law plant," he explained, "pretty to look at but full of thorns."

On these outings he would sing when we weren't talking. One of his favorite ballads included the line, "Yes, I know that all my life I won't be alone; someone will think of me a little; someone in this great immensity." He knew and loved every bit of the landscape. It was his hideaway, and he was willing to share it with this intruder and her dog. "Don't ever come here with anyone else," he warned. "This is my territory. I don't take you to nightclubs; I'm rough-hewn, and my world is here.

Aurelio's birthday fell on a Sunday in August. We went to one of his favorite places, where the sun filtered through the trees just enough to warm the grass without the air being too hot. I had brought an old quilt of my mother's for us to lie on and had a *pensierino*, an inexpensive gift, for him. We spent the afternoon there, relaxed and happy. But when I tried to give him the new wallet, he wouldn't accept it. His old one was worn through from sticking the metro, his folding meter measure, in his hip pocket. He made up excuses for not taking it, even saying that he had a new one in his dresser at home. He ended the conversation repeating that he had nothing to offer me, nothing but the work he could do with his hands.

Finally I made an awkward speech explaining why I could appreciate, respect, and love a man like him. It was true. I had grown up in a tiny, dusty town in Georgia where most of my playmates were barefoot farm children, many of them very poor. As a child I had lain on
the grass in silence, watching the stars; had walked in the woods, smelling the damp earth and listening to birds whose calls I couldn't recognize. Sometimes in the distance a guitar played romantic themes, probably strummed by an old black man on the porch of his shack beyond
the trees. I had loved escaping into nature. Then through my adult years I had seen a lot of high society, had met some of the rich and famous, and had performed on yachts in the Mediterranean and in Palm Beach, but I had never lost the memory of my childhood in the country.

I was at home with Aurelio because he was helping me re-evaluate my priorities, reminding me of my love of nature that had been misplaced or lost in the glitter of my social life. Together we could love and appreciate the simple things in life, the things that really count. My speech to Aurelio had an effect, and it served to help dissipate his feelings of my being too "high" for him, the term he used not sarcastically, but only as his reality.

10. IN THE OLD DAYS

The name Il Poggetto means "the little hill," a farmer told me, and is not an unusual name for a farmhouse in this area. The house originally belonged to the Fanelli family who still owned a fairytale castle in Sarteano. In the phone book their listing was "Fanelli, Fanello, Castello," and the number. Several rich families had built *palazzi* in the past centuries, but now these palaces had been divided into apartments of varying size and comfort. Some dwellings were three rooms, dark and damp, with no central heat and minimal sanitary necessities. Others, depending upon the way the sun hit them, were bright, airy apartments with loggias decorated with frescoes and views overlooking the countryside. Even the dingiest apartment nearly always had a tiny wrought iron balcony holding pots of geraniums or fuchsia and often with a canary in a cage, singing out in hopes of attracting a free-flying mate.

In 1617 Grand Duke Cosimo I (Medici) of Tuscany rewarded Eustacio Fanelli for his services to the state by giving him the Castle of Sarteano,which had been built in the 11th century. The castle had been renovated in 1575 and today in the 1980s remains in its medieval, though very much rundown, splendor.

The Fanellis owned a great deal of agricultural land. As was the system until recently, the feudal land was divided into *fattorie* – large, self-sufficient farm colonies – and every *fattoria* had its *poderi*, or individual farms, each with a *casa colonica* or colony house. The farmhouse of Il Poggetto had been a *casa colonica*, the whole property a *podere* belonging to the Fanellis. Self-sufficient, every *fattoria* had its own smithy, masons, and carpenters, all living on the premises with their families. An example of the enormity of some of these estates was near Sarteano. Named "La Foce", it is a *tenuta*, an estate, belonging to the Origo family. During the first half of the 20th century, La Foce grew to include fifty-seven *poderi* covering about 23,000 acres located in five different townships. Iris Origo, Anglo-American, in 1924 married an Italian nobleman, and the couple bought this large estate in the Val d'Orcia. Rather than live a life of luxury Marchesa Origo worked hands-on for the families, providing a clinic, one of the first Montessori Schools, and transportation, among other necessities that had been lacking for the farmers and their children. Her account of the war years, War in Val D'Orcia gives the reader a true sense of the hardships endured by every social class during World War II.

My five or so acres had been neglected for many years. The olive trees hadn't been pruned or fertilized for at least fifteen years, after the last family to occupy Il Poggetto had moved out. Raffaella sent her gardener, Carlo, to trim the trees. Carlo was an acquaintance of mine from the beginning as he worked nearly daily on Raffaella's property. He had been a mason but took early retirement because of a heart condition. He was good-natured, potbellied, deeply wrinkled, and toothless. He was always ready to join in conversation, especially while on the job for which Raffaella paid him the *lire* equivalent of $2.50 an hour. He was a hard worker, but he tended to pay attention to his favorite projects and neglect the other chores. He liked trimming trees as afterwards he could build a huge fire with the clippings. Often I was alarmed by the amount of smoke emanating from Raffaella's property, but Carlo kept the fires under control.

There was no question that my forty-two scraggly olive trees needed extensive cutting back. As they say here, "We're not trying to grow wood." The work ideally should have been done in spring before the new growth started, but I had been too involved in the house project to think of the land or trees. Trimming now in August meant fewer olives that first harvest, but healthier trees and a better yield in the future.

Carlo did the job, then a different man came and cleared the land around the base of each tree, and then Carlo put a chemical fertilizer around each plant, as the trees are referred to. Of course, I knew nothing about olive trees. Carlo said that I might have five or six liters of oil that first year, but that within a few more years the trees would give a big yield, perhaps 150 liters of oil. When I asked Carlo how old the trees were, he said proudly, "Centuries!" It wouldn't be time to harvest the olives until late November.

Several days later, Raffaella sent Carlo back to my property to burn the fallow fields. Carlo was eager to work for me and earn the extra income, and now he had a chance to build another bonfire! But Aurelio was taking more responsibility for the property, and he didn't want Carlo working for me. I didn't really need Carlo, who anyway was taking orders from Raffaella instead of from me. When Carlo began burning the first field, Aurelio said to me, "Go out there and tell Carlo to stop burning that field. This is your property, not Raffaella's." (Referring to Raffaella by her first name showed Aurelio's disrespect for her.)

This was exactly the sort of thing I was no good at doing, but I approached Carlo out in the field. "How's it going?" I asked with a smile. "Fine, Signora," he looked up at me; "this way the fields will be clean until next spring." "Actually," I said, "I've decided not to burn the fields this year. I'd like you to put out the fire and leave the fields as they are for now." Carlo was surprised, as clearly Raffaella had told him to come and burn the fields, and here I was telling him not to. Still, he tried at once to put out the fire, but it had already burned out of control and was heading for the property line and vineyard above my house. Realizing the situation, Aurelio and another workman ran to the field and beat at the flames until the fire petered out. Carlo and I remained on good terms.

Since I had not allowed Carlo to burn the fields, they needed to be cut. The wild flowers, leftover stalks of barley, and weeds in general were still waist high, inviting serpents and wild animals into the property. I was especially concerned about the presence of vipers as I had been warned that these poisonous snakes were aggressive and deadly. A viper's venom could surely kill Puffi and even a human. I had been ignorant of the danger the first time I came to Il Poggetto, had hiked up my dress, and had walked these same fields, proving myself a typical *americana*. Now Aurelio teased, "Don't worry, if a viper bites you, the viper will die." But it was Aurelio who soon found the man to cut the fields.

One evening an Ape came jolting up the driveway. From it emerged a large, solidly built man in his late sixties. "Signora," he announced, "I have come to see about the fields." His name was Bandelli, and he was to do the work assisted by his lanky, slow-witted son. In a few minutes Bandelli had surveyed by eye the land and could estimate the time it would take to cut the fields, bale the forage, and haul it away. As he studied the outside of the house, he surprised me by saying, "You know, I was born here."

In the mid-1920s, he had been born in what was now the upstairs studio. He told me that his family of six lived upstairs with the usual livestock downstairs. The farm had been one of the *poderi* belonging to the Fanelli family of the castle in town under the *mezzadria*, or sharecropping, system. The now fallow upper field had been a wonderful vineyard, there had been a vegetable garden and apiary on the south side of the property, and the olive grove had produced a rich harvest every autumn. The now-bedraggled walnut tree had been planted when Bandelli was three years old.

The lower field had always been sown with wheat or barley. He pointed out where the *aia*, the threshing floor, had been, about thirty feet from the house in an angle where the property was at its narrowest. He said that the old bread oven, built into the outside wall under the staircase, produced delectable foods, not only *pane* but roast goose and wild game as well.

In Bandelli's time there was no shortage of water, but it didn't come from a well. There had been two large tanks in back of the house that filled up regularly with the overflow runoff from town. That meant it was Sarteano's wastewater and undoubtedly stank, but it was good enough to keep the farm operating.

He confided that inside the kitchen wall there was "buried treasure," but I figured that he and his family would have taken it out before leaving the house for good. He added that if I were to dig around on the property I would certainly find Etruscan relics.

The people occupying these farmhouses were illiterate, but not to be underestimated. In Tuscany the farmers, the *contadini*, managed to grow olive trees at 1500 feet above sea level, then learned how to trim the trees to get a better yield of the precious virgin oil. These Tuscans had experimented with various grapes until they came up with Chianti, originally made of only Sangiovese grapes, then the blend of 70% Sangiovese, 15% Canaiolo, and 15% Malvasia grapes. This recipe was developed by

Baron Bettino Ricasoli, an important Italian statesman in the 1800s but with a keen interest in agronomy. His estate and castle in the heart of Chianti, Brolio, is where he worked on the grapes for Chianti, a wine first mentioned as far back as the 1300s. The ubiquitous straw-covered bottle, or *fiasco*, was not the baron's invention, having appeared in paintings by Ghirlandaio (1485) and Caravaggio (1595), but Ricasoli saw that it was a safer way to transport the bottles that were loaded onto ox carts then sent around the world via the high seas to places as far away as Bombay, where he exported his Chianti. This wine remains the best-known the world over.

Probably most influential in the lives of the *contadini* was the moon and its phases. The moon indicated when to trim the trees, when to plant what, when to graft the grapevines. Hair was cut when the moon waned. If a couple wanted to choose the sex of their longed-for child, it was enough to conceive when the moon was waxing to have a boy, waning for a *femminuccia*. Today most of the planting continues to be done according to the moon. If the weather in April is unseasonably chilly and rainy, the farmers will say, "It's still the March moon," rationalizing the late spring.

Along with the belief in witches, evil eyes, and ghosts, there was the Roman Catholic Church. The people mixed superstition with their religion. A sty was cured by pretending to sew it, needle in hand, while reciting an Ave Maria and Padre Nostro. The sty was punishment for a person who had eaten in front of the pregnant Madonna and not offered Her any of the food. Saint Helen was called upon to help find lost objects (Saint Anthony later usurped her position). Even Ciro, raised a Buddhist if anything, would cry out, "Saint Antonino" when looking for a lost object -- usually his glasses. On Good Friday special curative waters were collected that could heal any wound. Sarteano has a small chapel on the outskirts of town dedicated to the Madonna del Mal di Capo (Madonna of the Headache). It was said that any illness, but especially headaches, was cured in that chapel, and the stone wall is worn away where people have rested their foreheads to be cured.

These were the beliefs in the *mezzadria* system of farming. The landowner lived in his villa or castle, like the Fanelli family, and the *contadini* spent their lives doing backbreaking work only to give half their yield or more to the count or *marchese* or prince for whom they toiled.

Women, too, were in business selling eggs, chickens, *pecorino* cheese and other farm-raised goods. After the head farmer, the *fattore*, his wife was second in command and took charge with confidence when the *fattore* was absent from the farm.

In the *casa colonica* all activities centered around the kitchen, and that one room was referred to as the "house." The fireplace remained lit even in summer with the soup kettle hanging over the embers to help keep out evil witches. In winter the seniority of the two oldest members of the family earned them the right to sit on benches actually installed inside the hearth, and their food was kept hot on specially designed andirons that held the dishes chin high.

Nothing on the farm was wasted; manure, ashes and straw were all put to household use. If a pig was slaughtered, even its blood became scrumptious sausages or blood pudding. The farm women spun and wove cloth from wool or flax, braided straw into baskets or chair seats, and grew medicinal herbs. One weed, *erba di muro* that grew in the crevasses of the walls, had particularly sticky leaves so was used to clean out bottles.

Most of the medicinal cures were frightening concoctions made of pigeon waste, poisonous scorpions, thick blood from a wild hare, and horse urine. Among the cures, garlic was used in abundance, primarily for high blood pressure. The women would gather wild plants such as mallow for toothache and cultivated herbs like sage to treat such ailments as a sore throat.

One day Aurelio said that he needed to do something to soften his chapped, rough hands. "I know, I'll go out to the chicken coop and rub my hands in chicken shit, that'll soften them up." He looked at me out of the corner of his eye to see if I had fallen for his joke.

Having heard of the traditional cures, not to mention the lack of hygiene, I could well have believed him. Personal cleanliness was dismissed with, "*Tanto, in corpo c'é buio.*" (Anyway, inside the body it's dark). Bathrooms didn't exist, and rarely did the *poderi* have running water. Sometimes simply a hole in the floor of one of the upstairs human quarters opened onto the manure pile in the downstairs barn, serving as the toilet. It had been that way at Il Poggetto for the opening was still there when I purchased the house.

Only after the World War II did *mezzadria* begin to die out and with it the superstitions. But many of the strange beliefs still have an influence on the people. It is commonly accepted, for example, that if a person touches a snail and then with the same hand feels his own head, his hair will fall out. Figs, a September delicacy, are so highly prized that any malady that might strike a person in that season is likely to be blamed on having eaten too much of the succulent fruit. The illness, or bum leg, or inability to get pregnant, is rationalized as punishment for having pigged out on figs.

The history and tradition gave the people a provincial attitude; engagements were long, (often beginning, though, at a very young age). No one ever discussed how much money he or she had. But there was a perspective of time unknown to cosmopolites like me Work represented the most important factor in a man's life, but it got done at a slower pace (except for my roof). If

88

some trees didn't get planted this season, next year would be soon enough, as once planted they would remain there for centuries. When I lamented to Aurelio that I hadn't done any weeding in the small flower bed, he said, "*Piano, Susi*, you have all your life to do that."

It was the heritage of these strong and proud people, the history of Il Poggetto, that captivated me. I began to feel a part of it, as if my heartbeats, my joy, my pain, would be added to those who had lived here before me, and that my emotions would become part of the ancient walls, the fragrant earth. Clearly I could never become a *contadina*, as much as I admired and respected their simple qualities, nor could I even be Tuscan, but I could experience to the fullest the same feelings and could learn to appreciate the way these natives dealt with each other and with nature: the capricious seasons, the all-important crops, the people's lives together. Most of all, I wanted to live their way, according to their rules and values - assuming I could learn them. I had a long way to go.

11. THE *MATTI*

Sarteano shows physical traces of prehistoric man in the territory. But the first really great period occurred when inhabited by the Etruscans (Etrurians), at their peak about seven centuries before Christ. During their time the area was strong economically, and the people enjoyed the luxury of curative waters about which the poet Horace wrote. These Fontes Clusinae attracted tourists then as they do even today, reputed to cure diseases of the eyes and to alleviate skin ailments.

Between the second and first centuries b.C., the Etruscan civilization declined and was taken over by Rome, but it left behind innumerable underground tombs containing funerary urns of terracotta or marble with artifacts from daily life and often objects made of gold to help the deceased in the next life. Naturally, most of these tombs have been unearthed and robbed through the centuries, but now they are supposedly under the protection of the Italian government's Belle Arti.

Plenty of Sarteanans possess some sort of artifact: a water jug, a candle holder. One can imagine the treasures hidden away in cupboards to serve one day as a down payment on a new home or help in a geriatric crisis. The

Belle Arte cannot hope to put their hands on these closely hoarded family treasures.

Il Poggetto is situated in one of the richest Etruscan areas. The dirt road that passes the house was known until recently as the "road of the Etruscan tombs." Sometimes a workman at Il Poggetto will claim to be sensitive to the location of such tombs. One told me that there was a small tomb, "probably a child's," under my lone cypress tree. Another said that the front field was full of them, and indeed, true stories do exist of tractors sinking into tombs in a field that had been plowed and planted for centuries. Perhaps if I started digging surreptitiously I would end up with enough loot to support me in my old age, I fantasized.

Bardini, my closest neighbor beyond Raffaella, did just that. The loggia upstairs in my house overlooked his house and property. One night a bright light came through my upper story door, shining into my bedroom enough to awaken me. I heard large machinery of the *Catepilla* variety. Night after night the "ox eye" *occhio di bue* spotlight and heavy-duty digging continued. During the day silence prevailed, though enormous piles of earth were visible. Bardini was called a *tombaiolo*, someone who knew intuitively where Etruscan graves lay. He successfully dug only at night to avoid attracting attention. Inevitably, though, gossip started, but he had already accumulated much Etruscan loot. One man in town boasted that he had seen a statue a half-meter tall and of pure gold in Bardini's modest *casa colonica*. Carlo said that Bardini had been arrested at a police checkpoint on the *autostrada*, his Renault wagon filled with artifacts. Something did happen, for not long after the digging Bardini and his family no longer had green palor from starvation, and they sported new designer clothing. As solid as Cosa Nostra's *omertà*, my loyalty to Bardini meant that he and his family kept an educated eye out to protect me and my property.

Bardini could only be considered clever, almost a *mago*, a sort of Merlin, but my massive field hand Bandelli was harmlessly mad, and was referred to as one of the *matti*. As the shadows lengthened on my front field one warm afternoon, he began talking to me about his captivation with telling stories. Uneducated and ignorant of the world outside Sarteano, practically illiterate, he knew that there was no hope of getting any of his stories published. I wondered if his material might be good. When I asked him if his stories had fantasy, he proceeded to tell me one of them, neglecting his aching feet as he stood outside in the shade of the house.

He told of two *contadine*, two young farm sisters, circa 1915, one of whom had an especially pretty singing voice. One day while bathing in the nearby stream, ("They washed their hair with vinegar, Signora, I'll bet you never did that") the son of one of the local wealthy families heard the girl singing. Enchanted by her voice, the next day he called on her.

A difficult love story ensued, and perhaps Bandelli may have been writing it as he told it, but his innate consciousness and understanding of social prejudice, ignorance, and cultural differences made his story credible and interesting. His characters, so alive in his mind, became real to the listener as well. He had taken the tradition of storytelling around the fire in the evening and developed it into short stories, perhaps for a larger audience. I found it remarkable that this overworked, body-sore farmer had the compulsion and imagination to create stories.

When I mentioned Bandelli to a friend of mine in town, a native Sarteanan who was educated in Rome, she dismissed him with, "Oh, he's one of the *matti*. There has been so much intermingling of blood in this town that there is a high percentage of insanity." She went on: "Those who escape being crazy are particularly intelligent." In fact, I had noticed a larger than normal percentage of birth defects among the townspeople. There were, for example, various people with deformed or withered hands and arms. The Tuscan aphorism "*Mogli e buoi dei paesi tuoi*" (wives and oxen from your hometown) was a sentiment still taken seriously.

The Cat Woman was considered crazy, too. Married and with a family, this middle-aged matron spent hours every day feeding the hundreds of stray felines on the streets who had come to know her as their salvation. Fat cats, in fact, could properly describe these animals. Of course, it never occurred to the Cat Woman to have any of them sterilized so that no more unwanted kittens would be born. To her they were not unwanted! The woman covered on foot an area from the first square up all through the *centro storico* with its narrow, winding, hilly streets, on down to the local hospital.

The Cat Woman's routine, and one she never missed, was to collect food as she went along, give it out, collect from the next generous donor, give that out, and so on, so that she never had too much to carry at one time. Those housewives or restaurateurs who gave food were blessed by the Cat Woman, but woe to those who turned down this energetic feline lover. She gave them the human equivalent of a cat fight, spitting out vituperative language while barely losing a beat in her pace. She had a good seven miles to cover each day. The Cat Woman was unmistakable; always in a skirt and apron, she wore her graying hair in a charming topknot; and because of the miles she walked, she had the figure of a slim 20-year-old.

A sadder saga of the *matti* is told about a local man, Primo, the eldest of three brothers born during the fifties. As a youth this man excelled scholastically and was able to go to medical school, graduating with highest honors. Before settling down to a career as a physician in Sarteano, he and a friend decided to take an extended trip to Paris.

Long after their expected return, Primo appeared unannounced at the train station. On being interrogated he made no sense: he remembered nothing of his trip and had lost all rationality. His companion never returned. Primo, the promising doctor, took to wandering the streets of Sarteano, wearing the same heavy suit winter and summer, bumming cigarettes, often raving, totally mad. What happened in Paris remains a secret forever.

Various young people in Sarteano are mentally deficient, but harmless to society. They are neither discriminated against nor particularly coddled. At the newsstand one day, I saw one of these boys being reprimanded by the owner because he was swearing. "In my shop," she scolded him, "no one swears." Looking at her sheepishly, he shut up.

Unfortunately, these *matti* have no opportunities. There are no government-sponsored classes to help them learn a trade or to educate them to the extent of their abilities. They live at home or in an institution, their guardians receiving financial support from the State.

Most Sarteanans are cynical about life. "*La vita è una fregatura*" (life is a gyp) can be heard regularly in conversation. "*Siamo nati per tribolare*" (we are born to suffer) helps explain how life's pleasures come from simple things: good food, the teasing of one another, the satisfaction in children's accomplishments. Happiness is illusive, something for the rich. The Italian version of "born with a silver spoon in his mouth" becomes the working-class "born with a shirt" (*nato con la camicia*). "Good as gold" is rendered "good as bread" (*buono come il pane*). Priorities are realistic. Misfortune is to be expected; it is only a matter of time. Life offers endless hard work, dishonest government, and a guilt-provoking Catholic Church as Man's lot. These are some of the attitudes I learned about early on in Sarteano.

12. CONCERTS UNDERWAY

In midsummer of that year our first duo-piano concert was scheduled in Chartres, France, at the museum in the shadow of the world-famous Gothic cathedral. We were taking the train – starting from Chiusi, then changing in Florence to the overnight second-class *couchette*, a compartment sleeping six people. In Florence, we had nearly an hour's wait for the connecting train: Ciro disappeared to buy some Rocher chocolates, leaving me with the suitcases, briefcases of music, coats, a clothes bag with our evening wear, and a picnic of prosciutto, a slab of cheese, fresh bread, hard-boiled eggs, pears, and a bottle of Chianti. Our train arrived in his absence. Waiting for Ciro's return would have meant a last-minute scramble in the crowded train, so I had to load everything by myself, piece by piece, anxious that the luggage left on the platform might quickly disappear while I was on board positioning suitcases in the compartment.

Finally Ciro joined me on board, smiling as he carried his favorite chocolate: "Got it!" His boyish enthusiasm was contagious, and I knew the chocolate was excellent! Our compartment was full. A young French student who had been studying art restoration in Florence for years was going back home to Lille. Across from him was an American professor who spoke quite good French but no Italian. Completing the group was a mysterious, whispering, middle-aged couple who spoke Italian with a heavy German accent.

The day before we had left, my face broke out in a terrible rash. I thought it must be an emotional reaction to my involvement with Aurelio. As the train made its way north, my face became swollen, and the rash turned into fissures. Our travel companions were pleasant and not inquisitive; the conversation was minimal. Sleeping with strangers in such close quarters is always embarrassing, but Europeans acquiesce to the discomfort easily.

During the night Ciro made a scene. If he couldn't sleep, neither would anyone else. "There's no air up here; I can't breath," he complained in three languages. Up and down he went from his top bunk. I was so accustomed to such behavior from him that I didn't let it upset me; I didn't try to mollify the exasperated compartment-mates, who refused to allow the window to be opened more than a crack. I had my own problems with my boiling face. At last Ciro settled down, and the rhythm of the train lulled us.

We arrived in Chartres at noon the next day, met at the station by one of our sponsors, Monsieur Bonard. On seeing my face, he planted a wet kiss on the worst of the infection. Cheerily he drove us to the new hotel near the cathedral. I convinced Ciro that I needed professional advice about my rash. At a pharmacy the alarmed clerk gave me the name of a doctor nearby. He diagnosed a "microbe" that had invaded me and prescribed an antibiotic and several topical cures. The redness subsided almost immediately, but there was no way I could clear up the rash and ugly swelling in the 24 hours before our concert. Infact it lingered for over a week.

98

At the museum that afternoon, we found that the rectangular, mirrored room where we were to perform had no stage, but a platform had been built. We were given two good grands, a Steinway and a Kawai, on which to perform. The tuner was finishing up as we looked around the hall. There were folding chairs for about 200 people. We had to rehearse with the public on tour milling about, always a difficult and distracting task. We practiced using the microphones for our spoken introductions and my songs and went through all our numbers at an under-tempo, calm pace. After several hours we felt at home with the pianos and the room.

Dinner that evening was at the head sponsor's home in the country. The two-story house was built of red cedar that had been imported from Canada. Our hostess, Annie, was a delicate blonde, a pianist and singer who was French but had graduated from Vassar College. Her husband, Georges, was an internationally known artist whose stained glass creations were built into windows from Miami to Hong Kong. It was these kinds of patrons who made us feel nervous but who inspired us when we performed: fellow artists whom we barely knew, or worse, knew only by reputation.

Our program was out of the norm of the usual highbrow concerts presented by the Samedis Musicaux. The sponsors were taking a risk with our American program, so we felt all the more under pressure.
For the concert I wore an emerald green pants ensemble that I adored. It enhanced my figure, and it lent an informal tone to the evening. Ciro wore his usual midnight blue tux and red socks.

At curtain time we had standing room only. I felt in good shape emotionally and musically and had managed to layer my face with enough pancake makeup to cover the worst of the infection. Ciro felt nervous, but it was the kind of stress that helped him perform better.

It always happened that when one of us was nervous, the other somehow remained poised.

We received an enthusiastic reception from the minute we walked onstage. Every number went well: Gershwin's "Concerto in F," Ciro's interpretation of the "Rhapsody in Blue," and my two songs, "The Man I Love" and "Fascinating Rhythm." For the second half of the program, because it was July 4, we performed Ciro's "Yankee Doodle" caricatures, which included two which I sang, one in the style of Schubert with nonsensical German words, the other imitating Menotti's musical form with the words referring to some of the composer's operas. The public laughed and applauded on cue, and by the end of the evening everyone was pleased, especially, we were happy to see, the sponsors. Many new fans came backstage for autographs and hoping to buy tapes of the program, which we didn't have.

After a reception in the museum's garden, some old friends drove us to their unique home, a remodeled mill on the Avre River near Dreux. We enjoyed a relaxing, luxurious couple of days with Diana and Allen before the train trip back to Sarteano. Having triumphed in Chartres, we were already thinking ahead to our upcoming dates in Italy.

On our return Aurelio met us at the station in Chiusi. His face was flushed in anticipation, not only of seeing me, but because he had plenty to tell us, though none of it good. In our absence Gattone had ordered all the men to various other job sites: Aurelio was at a hotel in the hills, Nino and the others were working on an apartment house in town. Worse yet, Fabio was ill, and the youngest workman had broken his arm in a motorcycle accident. As Aurelio recounted these things, I found myself smiling in contentment as we drove up the driveway: I was back to my pleasantly familiar but problematic home.

In August Ciro and I were scheduled to give our

program as part of Sarteano's annual summer music festival. We had worked to convince the young and inexperienced festival director, a pianist himself named Zazzeri, to let us perform. The festival had rented only one grand piano, so we said that we would play on our own two uprights if the town would move them for us. The concerts were held in the Church of San Francesco, where every sound bounced around the stone walls. The only microphone available was the one don Paolo used to pray into; for my singing of the Gershwin numbers, the mike left a lot to be desired. We were determined, though, as Ciro rightly considered it important for us to become known in the community.

The day before the concert the town supplied us with movers and a truck, and our pianos were taken back down my exterior stairs and to the church. We rehearsed enough to get accustomed to the acoustics. There was a tuner on hand so we left the pianos to him. The concert was scheduled for 9:30, an hour that I couldn't get used to: it made the day of the performance such a long one.

From the beginning Aurelio had been against our performing in Sarteano, but he wouldn't tell me why. "I'll tell you after the concert," he had said. At 6:00 p.m., he came to wish me good luck. "*Auguri*," he said. "Leave your nerves at home." We puttered around the house doing small jobs as an excuse to be together. At 7:30 we were on the main road hanging a sign indicating the direction to Il Poggetto.

Aurelio had a precise understanding of my moods. Even when I tried to hide from him something that was bothering me, he never failed to ask what was wrong, and he wouldn't leave me alone until I had told him the problem. I knew he wasn't going to attend the concert, and it disappointed me terribly. But there was already gossip about us in town. Besides, he disapproved of our playing in Sarteano.

At 9:30 the church was packed, people sitting and standing in every available space. Gianmarco, the police chief, was in plain clothes in the front row along with a toupeed Gattone and his frilly wife. Nino and one or two of the other workmen could be spotted among the crowd. Besides local people, there were many tourists, mostly Germans who had attended the concert because they were Gershwin fans.

The evening was a huge success, so much so that envious Zazzeri hid us in the sacristy after our final bows and wouldn't open the door to let in the public. They found us, though, and lined up for autographs. Besides playing gratis and loaning our own pianos, I was chagrined at not receiving a bouquet of flowers from the sponsors, the first and only time in my career.

The next day when Aurelio came to see me, he had heard about our success. Nino had told him "They're international!" I asked Aurelio to tell me finally why he didn't want us to perform in Sarteano. "Because they don't deserve you here; they're ignoramuses." "In fact," I said a bit haughtily, "do you know that this is the first time I . . ." ". . . didn't receive any flowers," he finished.

Playing in the church was a far cry from the sophisticated performances we had given in the US. We had played over a hundred times at many private parties, in society mansions from Palm Beach to New York. I had enjoyed a personal success performing in front of producers and writers at the Dramatists' Guild above Sardi's Restaurant, and our program had become a tour de force. Sarteano offered a totally new and – it its own way – thrilling life, but it showed no resemblance to our professionally and socially successful background. My ambition was waning, my interests changing.

Though we had offered to play in Sarteano for nothing, a sort of gift to the community, Gianmarco felt responsible to find a way of repaying us. As police chief he had clout. He came to the house and asked us what we needed or wanted: a dishwasher? a refrigerator? After a few days' thought, Ciro decided on a dining room table. Gianmarco said fine, and he ordered a refectory table to be built by a local carpenter with the bill going to the town council. Thanks to Gianmarco's thoughtfulness and despite ulterior motives he had for me, we were given a solid oak refectory table, compliments of the Town of Sarteano.

The following Monday only the plumber and electrician were on the job downstairs. Then a day later, Aurelio and Nuccio returned to stay. Before we had gone to Chartres, one arch had been cut in a downstairs wall, and Aurelio had begun a second arch where a narrow door had led into the stall. The dirt and rubble had been cleared out, and some progress had been made in what was to become the kitchen. I still had no permit to remodel the downstairs. Gattone was getting nervous: "If we get caught working here without a permit, I'll go to jail," he warned. To make the crime seem less obvious, he continued to send only Aurelio and Nuccio to work; the other men stayed on their jobs in town. Progress slowed considerably, but without the permit, I couldn't argue with Gattone.

Early on, I had been advised of the *bustarelle*, the under-the-table payments made to high and low officials to get what one wanted. This was before Mani Pulite, the "clean hands" operation that brought worldwide attention to the corruption in Italian politics and business. The *tangenti* ran deeper than even the Italians had imagined. The idea of a *bustarella* was suggested to me when my request for the permit to remodel the downstairs was refused three times in succession. The permit had to come from a committee of eight regional bureaucrats. The committee head often influenced the others on the board by presenting a subjective view of the facts. Being a Communist and having a political appointment to the board, this man didn't want to help either a haughty noblewoman nor her American friend.

Raffaella had applied the first time for the permit even before my arrival on the scene. Decrepit Geometra Landi tried the second round and was denied in May. June went by with discussions as to why we continued to receive the *Nego* denial. The law said that on farmland, each piece of property had to maintain a lodging for domestic animals. In other words, it looked as if my planned living room, dining room, and kitchen had to remain available for livestock.

After spending August at the beach, Raffaella found us still cooking on the gas burner in the fireplace upstairs. Not one to hesitate, she accompanied me to the committee head's office in Montepulciano. I continued to be intimidated by her and felt like a puppy on its leash for the first time.

Raffaella had unsurpassed verbal skills. Not only did she talk a lot, but she also said a lot. Escorted into his stuffy, paper-strewn office, Raffaella was confident that she could handle this swarthy, small fry bureaucrat. "I have lived as ambassador's wife all over the world," she began, "and have been responsible for bringing many foreigners to visit Italy. This Signora has bought the *podere* next to mine in faith that she could restore and live in it. Being American she brings with her dollars and gives work to the local people. I find it embarrassing and unacceptable that your committee has refused her this building permit, and I shall write to my friend Minister Fanfani this very day to complain." Mentioning Minister Fanfani, a Christian Democrat in the Italian government since World War II, neither impressed the man nor helped my case. Raffaella's approach came from the old school of social and political hierarchy, telling off in no uncertain terms those beneath her – precisely the opposite line a Communist would sympathize with. And my being

American bringing "dollars with her" lowered the man's opinion of me. I was a capitalist pig being represented by a Catholic noblewoman. I should have taken Aurelio rather than Raffaella to convince this committee head! There were tears of frustration in my eyes as we marched out: Raffaella indignant and determined and I, having uttered not one word, feeling all the more defeated. Minister Fanfani did not respond to Raffaella's letter. Predictably the committee turned down the permit yet again.

During this period a matronly Florentine businesswoman, Carlotta, an old friend of Ciro's, happened to come for lunch. "The only way to get that permit," she asserted, "is with a *bustarella*. Don't come right out and offer money, but hint at it." Her eyes narrowed as she explained the intricacies of the operation. "If, for example, you discover that this man's son is about to be married, you might say, 'I think the couple should have a honeymoon in Florida, and I can arrange for their flights.'" Well, I had no intention of giving in to extortion to get what should by rights be mine. Besides, I couldn't afford such a *bustarella*!

Back to see Geometra Landi. By now he was beginning to feel that he had let me down. In my presence he phoned the same committee head. Il Poggetto and its 1.63 hectares were only a small piece of a larger property that had been owned by a local family before they had sold off the piece to me. They had retained the rest of the farmland. The phone conversation revealed that on the land from which my property had been extracted, there was a pile of stones that could legally be considered a barn. Eureka! My living room wouldn't have to house pet cows! I got the permit on August 25th.

Getting Gattone to send his men back to work at my house became the new problem. No longer having the excuse of no permit, he simply disappeared. I would go to the new job site in town to look for him, but he managed to dodge me every time. The men were glad to see me, though, and clearly they had less enthusiasm for the unimaginative job in town building a new *palazzo* than they had for their work in the country rebuilding my ancient house. The weather was hot, their work uninspiring, and the *operai* had no *bella signora* to boost their morale.

13. *FERRAGOSTO*

August in Tuscany brings pounding heat and
unrelenting drought. While May had been muddy, the
rain had ceased totally by June. Now the wheat was
dry, the sunflowers brown and drooping, and the earth
parched with inch-wide fissures. With no shutters on the
windows, my house welcomed the searing sun during the
day, refusing to allow us to nap. Even the nights meant
restless sleep with no air stirring. As for air conditioning,
local folks felt that it was a waste of money. It was enough
to know when to close and open the shutters to keep the
house cool in summer or warm in winter. My shutters
remained under the carport, waiting to be hung after
the house had been finished. I would have to postpone
learning how and when to open and close them. For now,
there was nothing to do but suffer through the heat until
the rains began again.

The week after our concert in Sarteano, all the
operai had their annual two weeks' vacation. Aurelio,
though, continued to come to work for me every day.
We painted the kitchen walls white and the beams and
crossbeams two different shades of brown. He hung the
mismatched secondhand aluminum kitchen cabinets.

Aurelio thought that I should be embarrassed at using old cabinets. He knew that Ciro and Raffaella had collaborated to get them, saving money as always. But the kitchen was the heart of the house and should have been given custom-made wood cabinets and new appliances. Beige wall tiles had been placed the end of July, and the old enamel sink, rescued from someone's backyard, had been installed with the tiles. I had found some used appliances at a reliable shop, so at last we could stop cooking in the fireplace upstairs. The final job was to install the one new and handsome article: a wrought iron light fixture, which Aurelio wired from the ceiling late the evening of August 14th. He worked by candlelight rather than have me go upstairs to get a flashlight, risking Ciro's curiosity as to what was going on. We admired the Tuscan fixture that hinted at what the kitchen's atmosphere should have been. "How can you invite people here with these cheap relics?" he asked, referring to the cabinets and appliances. He did not berate me, though, as he understood that I could not help but acquiesce to Ciro and Raffaella.

The next day, August 15, was the biggest summer holiday in Italy: Ferragosto, the Feast of the Assumption. In Sarteano it was celebrated with the re-creation of a medieval jousting match, with the competitors and their entourage in elaborate, colorful, heavy costumes inspired by the Renaissance. The match was called La Giostra del Saraceno. The Saracens were Arab invaders who terrorized a large part of Italy for centuries.

Historically, by the 6th century A.D., Sarteano was a fiefdom under the Lombards, who brought blond hair and blue eyes to the region; the Etruscans had been dark-haired with round, black eyes. These two strains are clearly visible in the current populace, with a mixture of Spanish features thrown in from when that army assaulted Sarteano in 1552. (Locally the Spanish word *mira* is used instead of the Italian *guarda* for "look.") Sarteano has been part of the Republic of Siena since 1467, so it was ruled by the Medicis during their long reign. The *giostra* replicated that era.

The irony in the behavior of the Tuscans, including the Sarteanans, comes at least in part from the both bellicose and intellectual natures of their forebears. The first governing Medici, Giovanni, gained power in Florence in the 14th century not by seizing it, but by helping to develop a democratic government which he then led. Lorenzo il Magnifico (1449-1492) ruled Florence and helped bring it into the Renaissance through his respect for learning and his patronage of the arts.

Later Medicis usurped more territory and power and became the despotic Granddukes of Tuscany, ruling until the family died out in 1737. The current Tuscan inherits his character from Dante and Michelangelo, but also from Machiavelli.

In the past 700 years Tuscans have been ruled by Muslims, Spanish, French, the Pope, and by each other. Today rivalry among the traditional enemies asserts itself in soccer matches, Siena's fierce Palio and our La Giostra del Saraceno. While the competition is serious, there remains room for jokes: "The Sienese snub the Florentines, the Lucchesi snub everybody." Sarteanans wish that the whole Italian peninsula south of their fair town would disappear into the sea, taking with it all its inhabitants.

It being my first Ferragosto in Sarteano, I wanted to participate in the festivities. Surprisingly, Aurelio had told me that he wasn't going; he didn't like crowds, he said. Ciro agreed to come along with me, and he brought a hot and uninspired Puffi on her leash. We arrived at the appointed hour, 3:00. I wore a cotton knit turquoise colored dress, hoping it would keep me cool. Nothing was happening yet; we had not learned that all public events began and ended late. Shutters were still closed, and people were not yet venturing out. We took our places in the main square and waited. By 4:00 the parade began to form, and the piazza was crowded with spectators.

Each neighborhood or *contrada* was represented by its jouster in the parade. All in renaissance-inspired costumes with the colors of the *contrada*, there were heralds in the form of a small drum corps, then the *contrada's* banner followed by several ladies-in-waiting wearing enormously heavy gowns and dragging plastic-lined trains. Escorting them were their cavaliers, a.k.a., the butcher, the deli man from the Coop, Felice, and my plumber. The jouster on his thoroughbred was last, and then there was a pause before the heralds announced the arrival of the next *contrada*. Somewhere in the parade was the local band, and the mayor and other dignitaries, all in costume, marched by. Every participant took his role seriously and made an impressive representation.

The point of the match was for each jouster on horseback to gallop towards the bust of a wooden Saracen whose arms were extended and who could spin around. At the end of one of his arms was a ring about four inches in diameter. The jouster tried to impale the ring with his lance as he galloped by. The competition was lively, and the winning *contrada* exulted until the *giostra* the following year.

The event was held on about 100 meters of straightaway on the newer main street in town, right in front of the Church of San Francesco. The pavement had been covered with a layer several inches thick of dirt and straw, and there were straw barriers on either side of the street. Bleachers had been set up along the route with standing room for those like us who bought general admission tickets. There were no concession stands or beer peddlers. No advertising was visible either along the jousters' route or among the public. Only homemade banners encouraging *"Forza, Mauro"* or *"Viva San Lorenzo"* could be displayed. Don Paolo blessed the riders and their horses, and the *giostra* was underway.

110

After about fifteen minutes, my two companions had seen enough and were ready to go home. Just at that moment I spotted Aurelio across the racetrack, and he saw me. He came over and stayed with me while Ciro and Puffi went back to the car. Aurelio explained about each jouster's abilities, gossiped about how much money each was paid for the event, about his love life, and about other facts of his life outside the Ferragosto festivities. Soon Ciro came back to get me, so I did not see either the winning race nor the awards ceremony.

The next day I heard from Aurelio that after the match the winning *contrada* had celebrated far into the night. The women from the neighborhoods that didn't win had come looking for the women of the victorious sector, and there had been a free-for-all female fistfight that had turned into a tearing-off-of-clothes display. The men had stood and ogled. This behavior by the women was not held against them and was forgotten in a couple of days – so they said.

Every year for several weekends prior to the *giostra*, each *contrada* offered an outside supper of local specialties. The food was good, the local wine pure, and the townspeople enjoyed being outdoors and in each other's company. There was a band for dancing; the evening didn't end until way past midnight. Biggest of these events was the Communist-sponsored Festa dell'Unità, but my favorite was that hosted by the local hunters' association, ARCI-Caccia.

I had never condoned hunting, and this so-called sport was hotly contested even in Italy. Italian hunters killed songbirds – skylarks, blackbirds, even robins – and in many instances had decimated various indigenous species. There were so few pheasant left that they had to be imported from Eastern Europe. The native Tuscan pheasant became extinct. The laws had been written under Mussolini's dictatorship, spurred by both nationalistic machismo and by the basic need for food in those days. But the laws were changing, and there was even a movement to suspend hunting for five years, giving the prey a chance to repopulate. The hunters realized that after the five-year moratorium it would be difficult to get hunting reinstated, so the movement was squelched before it could be passed into law.

The hunters, including Aurelio, who sponsored and cooked for the dinner, though, were members of ARCI-Caccia, most of whom had respect and love for the animals, the land, the conservation of flora and fauna. The men thought of themselves as environmentalists. They adhered to the hunting laws, which admittedly were lax. It was their irresponsible counterparts who damaged the name of hunting in Italy: those who hunted in groups with too many dogs, used captured birds as prey to attract other birds, and shot at anything that moved in the forest – all illegal actions. Every year there were instances of hunters who mortally wounded someone's grandmother who was in the woods searching for *porcini* mushrooms. The hunters mistook even one another for a wild boar or a deer in the bush, largely because the accepted attire for hunters was khaki green. No red jackets or bright orange ponchos for these machos!

Hunting season in Tuscany opened the third Sunday in September and ended the last Sunday in February. On that warm Sunday of opening day I hardly dared open my door to go outside. Hunters had camped out all night to reserve their favorite site. Shooting began at dawn and ended at sunset, and the pheasant who had visited my property since spring were shot before I had had breakfast. The hunters were supposed to keep 100 meters from any dwelling, but plenty of shots rattled my windows, and once I even got sprayed with 20-gauge shot. Every man or woman who ever went hunting was out on that first day of the season.

112

The hunting season for some quail, partridge, and pheasant lasted several months, but a shorter season limited the killing of animals such as ducks and wild boar. The boar, a ferocious beast that destroyed agriculture, had to be hunted by groups of men who surrounded it, then sent in their ruthless dogs who often got badly gored by the tusks. During the wait, the hunters could not move, smoke, talk, or pee, as the boar were so sensitive to any change in the surroundings. Finally, *palottole* the size of a large man's thumb were fired into the one or several cornered boar.

At the dinner sponsored by the hunters, my favorite dish was tagliatelle with wild boar sauce. The sauce was rich with the gamey flavor of the boar, mellowed with garlic, rosemary, fresh peeled tomato, red wine, olive oil, and plenty of salt. It was a *casalinga* sauce; it had a country flavor, rough and unrefined, that represented the area and people of Sarteano.

Besides the specialty of boar there were quail roasted over an open fire, grilled steaks and chops, and homemade sausages with fennel served with cannellini beans. All the food was prepared on the spot in the town park. A shack with walls of *canetti* (reeds) served as the kitchen, and a huge grill near it had coals kept alive for days. Wooden tables and benches were placed in uneven rows, and naked light bulbs were hung giving a garishly festive brightness. Food was paid for at a small table manned by Felice, then patrons lined up to be served their dinner hot off the grill and straight out of the cooking pots. Most people knew to bring their own trays. The fragrances permeated the air during these days and made our mouths water. Aurelio worked for four nights cooking, nursing the sauce, stirring and serving. He wore my beige neck scarf in the breast pocket of his green sport shirt. Although no one knew what it represented or who its owner was, he showed it off proudly as if it were a medal.

Even though these dinners were held at the height of the tourist season, few outsiders attended them. It was just as well, for these relaxing evenings served as a breather for the locals who, taking advantage of the lucrative summer season, had to put up with the demands of badly dressed campers who for the most part spoke no Italian but knew how to insist on what they wanted from the merchants. Instead the townspeople ate heartily at the dinners then danced to romantic tunes of the '50's, such as *Tango dei Capineri*.

Despite Sarteano's economic success through its beneficial waters and agricultural strength, the 19th century brought a crisis: the railroad was built 10 miles away. No longer on the main road to anywhere and too far from the railroad to be feasible, the town began to suffer economically. With the end of the feudal *mezzadria* and the growth of industry after the Second World War, Sarteano lost over a fifth of its population. In an effort to recuperate, the town tried to develop tourism, thus providing jobs and giving an incentive to its youth to remain in their simple hometown. But the town fathers hadn't come up with a good plan for attracting more tourists – their hopes were in the campground and swimming park with its special waters plus the *giostra* – but increasingly the young people were forced to go elsewhere to find work.

The future for Sarteano's children held little promise. Most high school graduates did not go on to university, despite being state-run and costing little. Those who did get a higher education moved on to urban centers where jobs were more likely to be available. The young people who stayed in Sarteano had career opportunities only if there was work via a family member: if Babbo had a car dealership, or if Zio had his own construction company. A few of the high school graduates took courses to become CPAs or computer technicians, then found the

114

market flooded when they job hunted.

Most job offers in Italy are made by way of a *concorso*. These competitions, announced well in advance to the public, require a participation fee of $50 to $100. As the *concorso* is held only in one city, the applicants often travel by train overnight, arriving tired and hungry just in time for the exam. Thousands show up. The announcement of 1,000 openings for a highly coveted State employment position brought 40,000 participants to the exam, not an unusual turnout. During the seeming impartiality of these competitions, nepotism, bribery, and sexual favors are ways of securing the job. Once inside the system with a *raccomandazione*, careers move ahead automatically.

I became acquainted with a young woman who graduated from a prestigious Tuscan music conservatory. She was a flutist of great merit, but at 23 had all but given up hope for a career. She was not aggressive (she was an artist!) and had no useful contacts to help her get accepted into an orchestra. She worked for her father in the local camera shop in town and waited tables for fussy tourists in Chianciano in the summer.

Often the local girls passed the time at some uninteresting sales job until their boyfriends got them pregnant. They married and settled down to their predictable lives, frustrated that they were unable to break away even briefly from their provincial destinies.

The relationship between mother and child formed the core of the lives of these people. Fathers were rarely on the scene except to eat and sleep and had little to do with the children's upbringing. But the mothers shared every secret, every emotion with their children. *Fai la tua* (mind your own business) was the posture given outsiders, but children confided everything to their mothers, knowing that they would receive help and support no matter what.

"Mamma, I'm going to spend the night at Gianni's house," an 18-year-old girl would say. "*Si*, Cara, phone me when you get there," responded the mother in all tranquillity. Parents assumed as natural the sexual appetites of their children of a certain age. Gianni, of course, was the girl's steady boyfriend, her *fidanzato*, whom she would marry eventually.

Sons felt the absence of their fathers, and when they were embarrassed to confess everything to their mothers, they found a substitute in the grandfather or a close older friend. The male role model would have been the adored father if he were ever home. It was not that the fathers didn't love their children; they had grown up with an absentee father and didn't know how to stay home and participate in family life. I asked Aurelio, "Did you ever feed one of your children when they were babies?" "I think I remember doing it once – *Che disastro!*" he remembered.

Carlo, the firebug, had a son and daughter-in-law who created an enormous scandal in town: they started divorce proceedings. Not only did a divorce take a minimum of three years and millions of *lire* in attorney's fees, but also, very simply, no one ever divorced in Sarteano. This couple had married in their teens, had a son, then found irreconcilable differences as soon as they reached their twenties. Having a lover was considered the norm, but marriage was a bond not to be broken under any circumstance save death. I was acquainted with married couples who did not speak to one another though they lived in the same house, couples who were never seen together in public, who had nothing to do with their respective in-laws. Legally, though, their marriage was intact, so all was well. This tradition came not only from the Church, but also from the State: as recently as the 1970's, divorce was illegal in Italy, and one could go to jail for committing adultery.

116

14. INJUSTICE PREVAILS

Sometime during this period, Aurelio decided that I had better meet his wife. I knew that he had two grown children and that his parents lived in the same house with his family. He cautioned, "*Sono gelosi di me*," meaning that his parents were jealous of any time or commitment he gave to others.

One afternoon he wanted to help me go and choose downstairs floor tiles. Ciro was busy as usual, so he didn't mind my going off with Aurelio. Before leaving for Chiusi, Aurelio needed to change out of his work clothes. "I can't be seen like this in the company of a *signora*," he said. We went to his home so he could change. He lived in a fairly new two-story stucco house in town. His parents occupied the ground floor; he and his family lived upstairs. We greeted his parents first. Aurelio's looks had come entirely from his mother: the well-formed nose, the green eyes. Both his parents were cordial and clearly proud of their only child.

Aurelio took me up the exterior stairs to his apartment. There was a dark entrance hall, a bathroom straight ahead, three small bedrooms, a centrally located modern kitchen, and an overcrowded living/dining room off which there was a tiny balcony. Two female voices came from behind the closed shutters of the balcony door. Aurelio said that his wife was out there with her sister and called to the wife to come inside.

The *operai* rarely spoke of their wives. The only thing I had heard Aurelio say about his was that she was "old." He had told me that as a young man he had been a carefree bachelor, but that his parents had prodded him into getting married so that he wouldn't be alone in his old age. At that time, when he was 25, he worked in Switzerland and came back to Sarteano only for Christmas and a short summer vacation. He was girl crazy and had passionate adventures going on -- several at a time. Graziella was the one he married because he got her pregnant. They were married in Sarteano, but he continued to work in Switzerland until after his second child, his son, was born, when he moved back to Sarteano.

Aurelio had told me that even after his marriage he never gave up the other women, and after 25 years the story hadn't changed. He never had what was considered a mistress, one woman with whom he had an ongoing relationship. His were always today this one, tomorrow another, until I appeared on the scene. I imagined his wife as a smiling, petite, dark-haired woman with nice features and a soft-spoken manner, happily married to the man she loved and self-confident enough not to feel threatened by his sexual shenanigans.

Aurelio had told me from the beginning three months earlier, practically with the first kiss in the damp stall at Il Poggetto, that he would not divorce his wife. I understood that this was a traditional Tuscan response to a common situation. In America where an unfaithful spouse was often the reason for divorce, here divorce was considered more scandalous than a love affair. My reaction to his unequivocal statement was that I had to abide by the ways of my adopted country. My feminist

118

sense of independence helped me overcome any hurt pride.

Aurelio tolerated his wife and was devoted to his children, so his life had gone on in a routine of lots of work, casual sex, and family. He still went hunting with his father and often ate downstairs with his parents rather than upstairs with his wife and children. Graziella had always worked, too, having been brought up in postwar Italy where a mentality of conspicuous consumption reigned, and money was necessary. Aurelio's father had his pension and had helped pay for the house, so with several incomes they all lived comfortably though not luxuriously.

All this was running through my mind as I prepared to meet Graziella. What I hadn't anticipated was that she would look like a giant panda. A half-foot taller than Aurelio, she weighed over 200 pounds, had cropped, frizzy, dyed brown hair, false teeth, and bruise-dark skin under her eyes. As she reached out to shake hands with me, I couldn't believe what I was seeing. "This is my wife," Aurelio said, and his eyes added, "Now you see what I live with."

While Aurelio changed clothes, I sat with his wife and her sister on the balcony. Graziella didn't dream that I, a *signora*, in a social class well above theirs, would be interested in her husband outside his role as workman. I never did so much talking, and in Italian, as on that balcony. I described Florida, I enthused about Il Poggetto, and I told them about Ciro and our concerts . . . Aurelio was taking forever to change. After what seemed like an entire afternoon, he reappeared and we could leave. I felt like Jane Eyre and could think of nothing to say to Aurelio. Luckily he and his father had shown me the vegetable garden and cellar with the *prosciutti* hanging from the beams and, of course, I had met both his parents, so in the car I talked about everything at his house except Graziella.

I realized that what Aurelio had said was true for him – that I was "a rose among thorns," "*perfetta*," as he described me. Even Ciro observed that Aurelio looked at me as if I were a fairy princess. My self-esteem had been beaten down to the point that I couldn't imagine anyone finding me pretty or bright or even interesting. Aurelio saw me as beautiful, intelligent, and fascinating. Together we were building a relationship that fit somewhere between fantasy and Tuscany.

Gattone wanted to cut corners as much as possible, even to the extent of abusing the building code. For example, because Il Poggetto was in an earthquake zone, two steel beams had to be put over every door as a safety measure. According to the code, once they were in place these three-sided beams were to be filled in with concrete. Plastered over, no one could tell whether or not the beams had been filled. Gattone told the men not to fill the beams. I was oblivious to these shortcuts, but Aurelio and Gattone would get into ferocious arguments with lots of swearing and name-calling. Aurelio was sensitive and hated confrontations, but when necessary, he didn't shy away from them. Gattone would get his way by making sure that Aurelio was working on a different project than the one involving the shortcut, but invariably Aurelio would find out what was going on at Il Poggetto and come to my defense. I kept Gattone on rather than firing him because of Aurelio. If I had broken the contract, I could never have compensated for Aurelio's personal interest and help in rebuilding the house.

Aurelio had worked for Gattone for fifteen years, even through the bad times when Gattone had declared *bancarotta* in the 1970s. In Italy a workman such as a mason could retire after thirty-five years of service, and Aurelio had just one year to go when I met him, even though he was only fifty years old.

Late one foggy evening, we went to the union office to find out exactly when he could begin collecting his pension. "For a year," he told me in the car going to the office, "I could even spend the time in jail. When the day comes I'm going to get drunk with my father." But when we got to the union office, there was bad news. Gattone had failed to pay in his contributions towards all the men's pensions during the period in which he had gone bankrupt. Aurelio would have to work for nearly four more years to compensate for the missed payments. There was no insurance for cases like Aurelio's, and Gattone had seen to it that he had no property in his own name, having put it in the name of the frilly fluff of his wife. Suing him, therefore, would bring nothing.

The following day I felt indignant enough to go by myself to the police station to complain to Gianmarco about this injustice to all Gattone's workmen. Gianmarco said, "Don't worry about the *operai*; these workers have a good life." "But isn't there some way of getting them the money they earned?" I persisted. "They have all filed charges against Gattone," yawned Gianmarco, "but he has nothing in his name, so nothing can be collected. Even if Gattone's few possessions were auctioned there wouldn't be enough to pay one man, certainly not the six *operai*" I thought, "Is it any wonder these workers are card-carrying Communists?"

As the months went by that first year in Sarteano, I lost interest in performing on stage; its glamour seemed superficial to me now. I had no more desire to travel, whereas for many years my peripatetic inclinations influenced my desire to be a performer. Most of all, though, I found that I could no longer tolerate living with Ciro. What had kept us together the past five or six years had been our mutual musical interests. Now, though, there was not even that to help keep intact a languishing relationship. We were so close, spending nearly all our time together, that he once said, "Making love to you would be like making love to my sister." The lifestyle that had attracted me to him – society, sophisticated conversation, and the travel – paled in comparison to the simple, natural life I now embraced.

Ciro saw my transformation, but he didn't want to believe how much I was changing and how foreign it was to our former life together. He became jealous of Aurelio. When Aurelio discovered that Ciro was suspicious that we were having an affair, Aurelio confronted my husband in front of the fireplace late one afternoon. "I am fifty years old," asserted Aurelio. "I am married to a woman I admire and have two children whom I adore. I don't come here to take advantage of the *signora*. I come here to work because I see that you need help. If I wanted, I could find plenty of girls in town to fool around with." Ciro was convinced. Aurelio had made this speech in front of me, and I was amazed at his acting ability. Then I realized that what Aurelio had said was true; he did admire his panda wife and love his children. He wasn't taking advantage of me, and I wasn't just another woman with whom he was having a fling. And in addition, no one recognized more than he that we needed help with the house.

Aurelio had told me from the beginning of our relationship that he would be devoted to me and do all he could for me, but that he would not divorce or even separate from his wife. He understood, too, that I was coming out of a stifling marriage. He said, "You must be free from now on." Though we loved being together, each of us knew how important independence was, both to the health of us as individuals and to that of a close relationship. A few times he asked me, "*Mi vuoi sposà'?*" But whether I said yes or no to his marriage proposal, we both knew it was at best truth in jest.

At the end of August thunderstorms brought deliverance from the heat and relief to the parched land.

Aurelio announced, *"E' finita l'estate!"* (Summer is over!) In September, work at Il Poggetto moved at a slow pace. Aurelio had made a niche in what was to be the downstairs bathroom, thus providing enough space to put in a bidet as well as a shower, sink, and toilet. The niche had been a big project because it meant breaking through a wall and then building a new, thinner wall in its place.

The distraction of my presence didn't help him get the work done but he wanted me by his side every moment even if I wasn't able to help him. "Do you want something to drink?" I would ask mid-afternoon. "I want you," he would reply. Every work gesture was punctuated by a kiss, a caress, a teasing remark. Seeing my red toenail polish, he frowned. "Aw – how did you cut your toes?" He sang from his vast repertoire of love songs: "I'll never leave you. You are the queen, and I am your king." "I'm sure in this great immensity someone will think a little bit about me, will not forget me. I know that all my life I won't be alone." Our bond was growing, our devotion to each other stronger.

What had been the stable in the house remained entirely as it was except that it got cleaned out. The floor was still dirt, the walls had not been plastered, the pipes and wiring had not been laid, and the windows were still original -- small, round openings like portholes. Finally, shy Calvi brought the new door for the stall. It was an antique wrought-iron piece that I had ordered be fit with thermal glass from top to bottom. The door was divided into two panels, each of which could be opened, and it measured about four feet wide by seven. Once installed, it let in glorious sunshine and gave a view of my south field, then Monte Cetona then the restored monastery beyond. The stable door was installed while we were an hour's drive away giving a concert. I resented having to leave while this work was being accomplished, but at least we weren't going far, and I was so comfortable with the program that there was no problem with nerves.

15. MORE CONCERTS . . .

This concert was at Gargonza, a medieval castle complex near the Tuscan town of Arezzo, owned and operated by a true nobleman, Count Guicciardini. He had made his property into an international conference center. One time it would be full of Germans, another time English. Besides the former watch tower, which the Count used as his overseeing residence, he planned that there would be various small stone houses and remodeled apartments for the guests, plus assembly halls and a paved courtyard with its original well, all within the castle walls.

For several summers, Gargonza sponsored Sunday afternoon concerts. Usually the artists were from the conservatory in Arezzo. The Count was not enthusiastic about an all-Gershwin program; he felt that Gershwin's music was too jazzy and, therefore, inappropriate to the atmosphere at Gargonza. But Richard and Kenneth, American friends of ours who lived near the castle and friends of his, convinced the nobleman to let us perform, even though it meant bringing in a second grand piano to accommodate our needs.

Our concert was scheduled for 6 p.m. in a hall that held about 150 people, and it was sold out. While nearby townspeople were invited to attend, most of the audience was made up of guests at the castle, who happened to be English on this particular day. The remodeled hall had an excellent overhead lighting system, and the sun poured through the windows as well. We didn't need microphones. With ample rehearsal time, all went well after Ciro insisted that yes, there was room on the temporary platform for both pianos. We were beginning to feel confident about the program, having given it several times, and this concert was easier, being at a relatively early hour.

Richard and Kenneth invited us to spend the day of our performance at their country home nearby. That meant we could have a leisurely lunch then rest before leaving for the castle. Our friends were always gracious and relaxed and amused us with gossipy stories of mutual friends and acquaintances. We enjoyed passing the time with them before our 4 p.m. scheduled departure. They would be joining us later to hear the program.

As usual, I drove Ciro and me in the blue Fiat. As I pulled out into the long, winding dirt driveway, Kenneth called out, "You can take a shortcut, but be careful of the ditch in the field on your way." The shortcut looked easy, as the field had been recently cut. I took off with confidence when KLUNK! – the car hit the ditch head first. There was no way of backing or moving forward. Ciro started raving as we got out of the car and walked back to the house: "What have you done! I bumped my head – you could have killed me! Don't you know I have to play a concert today?" Richard and Kenneth witnessed the whole scene and took it calmly except for Ciro's overreaction. Didn't I have to play the concert, too? With a phone call Richard found a neighbor who kindly pulled the Fiat out of the ditch with his tractor, and we were back on our way in plenty of time.

For this concert, Ciro wore a white suit, good-looking but of very heavy material, and he began sweating even before the performance. I wore red silk pants and a matching blouse. Pants were becoming a trademark; I was so much more comfortable and at ease in them after years of performing in stiff gowns.

We opened the sold-out program with Gershwin's "Concerto in F." The end of the first movement is exciting, thrilling both listener and performer, and we were giving it our all. As the last chord was played, an English woman on the front row cried out, "My God!" It never failed that we got applause after that first movement out of inevitable enthusiasm for the brilliant music.

All was going well until the sun slid just far enough to come through the window behind me and then hit Ciro smack in both eyes. Already he was a river of perspiration in that suit, and now he was being blinded by the sun. Since there was no intermission, I wanted to do something to lighten the situation. As he was introducing "An American in Paris," both of us standing in front of the pianos, I knew that he would explain about the French taxi horns. When he reached that point in his monologue, I chimed in with an imitation of the horns: "beep-beep-beep, bup-bup-bup," on two vocal notes. Ciro was charmed by my improvisation; he relaxed and afterwards said, "Keep it in!" I did my taxi-horn solo from then on.

Richard and Kenneth joined in the boisterous applause when we finished the program. The flowers offered me were red roses straight from Gargonza's garden, presented by the Countess. It was a touch that went well with the atmosphere of that remote castle.

We returned home the same evening only to take off again two days later to a concert much further away. Sorrento, on the coast near Naples, was a place we had visited before. This time we were to give a concert there at the Teatro Armida. A good friend of ours from Florence,

Marisa, offered to drive us down and back in her big, low, blue Citroen. Marisa's sister lived near Sorrento, so Marisa could spend with her the two nights we needed to be in Sorrento. It was a long drive, toll road all the way, meaning that to keep up with the traffic one had to drive at least 80 miles an hour.

Marisa had been a great beauty in her youth, but working in tomato fields developing new hybrid seeds plus adding too many extra pounds through the years had robbed her of much of her physical appeal. She had not lost the best of her attributes, though: her intelligence and good humor made her a pleasure to be around. With an intense interest in many subjects and in every person she met, with her excellent Italian pronunciation and her marvelous sense of humor, she had given me some of my best days in Italy.

During this trip to Sorrento, she trusted me (but not Ciro) to drive part of the way. While I was at the wheel I asked her to share some of her experiences as a little girl during World War II. Many Italians had heart-rending stories about the War, and Marisa recounted hers with clarity and deep emotion without being maudlin.

She told of the time when she and her family had practically nothing to eat and had had nothing for months. Marisa was about ten at the time, the middle daughter, and her body suffered from not only hunger, but from malnutrition. One day she was out running an errand for her mother. "I was barefoot all the time and had calluses thick as bottles on my feet," she explained. She only was allowed on the deserted streets because her older sister was already a *signorina* and couldn't go out alone, and the younger sister was too small. As Marisa hurried home from her task, suddenly standing before her was an American GI, a big, husky black man. She had never seen either an American or a black man before. He leaned towards her and gave her a broad, sparkling smile.

Marisa stood frozen with fear. The soldier handed her a thick slice of white bread slathered with honey. White bread had not been seen in most of Italy for years; only coarse, dark bread might be available on rare occasions. Marisa, torn between paralyzing fear and agonizing hunger, finally grabbed the bread and ran home as fast as she could. She gave the bread and honey to her mother, who divided it into equal portions for each member of the family, but Marisa couldn't eat her piece. The experience had been too traumatic.

Listening to Marisa made the trip pass quickly. We went to her sister's house first to pick her up, then on to Sorrento. In Sorrento the traffic wasn't moving. It was hot, we were tired, but there was nothing to do but wait to inch a little farther down the street. Suddenly, on a small billboard, I saw a poster announcing our concert the following evening. This sight brought us back to life and actually impressed Marisa and her sister. They dropped us at the hotel and left immediately as they wanted to stay out of our way. We would see them after the concert.

Our corner room in the hotel was on the top of the five floors in the four-star hotel. The room itself was small, but we had two balconies – one overlooking a park, the other with a spectacular view of the Bay of Naples and Vesuvius. For all our concerts the sponsors gave us the best accommodations available and treated me like a diva and Ciro like a great maestro.

After a good night's sleep, the next morning we walked to the Teatro Armida where we were to perform that evening at 8:30. Now a movie theater, the Armida seated about 800 people downstairs and perhaps 400 more in the balcony. The stage was enormous and clearly had been home to lavish theatrical productions in the past.

There were six men working onstage. The pianos had arrived but were not in place yet. The men were concentrating on setting a bank of overhead lights for us, but Ciro interrupted their work and tried to make them put the pianos in place so we could begin rehearing. The men didn't approve of Ciro telling them how and when to do their work, and they nearly walked out on us. I intervened and tried to make Ciro realize that it was early and that we could perfectly well rehearse in an hour rather than at that precise minute. That's how we resolved the situation; and when we returned at noon the lights were set, the pianos were in place, and the men were gone. After working with the lights and microphones and having run through the program slowly, by mid-afternoon we felt all was under control.

The balcony was closed off for the concert, and rightly so, as no one could estimate what the turnout might be; also, those seats were very far from the stage. The concert was offered free to the public, sponsored by a local cultural group, and had been well publicized, so we expected a good crowd.

We arrived back at the theater at about 7:30. The dressing rooms were in the traditional style: several small rooms, each with a large well-lit mirror, some hooks to hang clothes, and a sink with cold running water. I dressed in my emerald green pants outfit and put on my stage makeup and was ready by 8:10.

Ciro told me to go out and look from behind the curtain at the hall. I saw three people in the audience. I went back to the dressing room and wrote a postcard to my parents. Ciro and I were accustomed to the public arriving at the last minute, but when at 8:25 there were only twelve people out there, we got nervous. It was unbelievable. "How can it be with all the publicity they gave us? Don't these people like Gershwin?" asked Ciro incredulously. His voice was frantic. At 8:35 there were fifteen souls in the audience. Ciro said to me, "Well, we're here to give a concert; let's go on." We went to the stage manager and told him we were ready. "It's a little early, don't you think?" he asked calmly. "We've waited until 8:40, but now we'd better get started," Ciro said. "But the program isn't scheduled to begin until 9:15," the stage manager informed us. At 9:15 there were over 700 people in the audience. Ciro was able to laugh afterwards, but he had been dumbfounded at the idea of our concert not attracting a full house.

After the performance, Marisa and her sister rushed backstage, full of enthusiasm and gushing about the concert. There was the usual line of autograph seekers, something that always thrilled me, for as a little girl I had been a keen collector of the signatures of people who led what seemed to me like such glamorous lives.

Later, after the fans had gone, our sponsors took us to dinner at an intimate restaurant nearby. We were ten people and highly visible in the small dining room, dressed as we were and with me carrying several large bouquets of flowers. Other customers stared at us, wondering who these celebrities might be. In a corner of the restaurant I spotted Robin Williams, the actor/comedian. He attracted no attention and his foursome had a quiet, romantic dinner. As they got up to leave, Robin's wife was walking in front of him. He patted her bottom and said, "Yum,yum."

The next morning various hotel guests stopped to congratulate us, and at breakfast in the dining room I could see we were whispered about. If nothing else people always remarked on our age difference, usually with innuendoes. As we were loading Marisa's car to leave, a young woman came running towards us carrying a large potted philodendron. "At last," she gasped, "I've found you. I'm a music student and love jazz, and your concert was the best thing I have ever heard . . ." The philodendron was taken back to Il Poggetto to delight us.

Next was Arezzo. Here we had been told that critics from the press would cover the concert. The theater was part of the conservatory in the heart of the old section of Petrarch's hometown. The pianos were excellent, and the hall held about 400 people.

There were two dressing rooms, but neither had even a sliver of a mirror, nor did the bathroom, so I had to put on my stage makeup using a compact mirror that I happened to have brought. This evening Ciro was back in form, and Richard and Kenneth were again in the audience to bolster our courage.

The program began well. Good pianos are always inspiring, and we had an SRO audience of mostly students. In the second half of the program, just before my Gershwin songs, some of the lights went out. We lost our spots, all backstage lighting, and worst of all, both microphones went dead. The sponsors stopped the show momentarily, but the problem could not be fixed immediately. I indicated to the audience that I would need total quiet to sing, implying that otherwise they wouldn't be able to hear me. In reality, I didn't need the mike, and the songs went over extremely well because of the added drama. My voice was unexpectedly loud and clear, surprising me more than anyone else. The critics wrote very complimentary reviews, including that I sang with "*disinvoltura*", that is, free and easy.

As my self-confidence on stage increased, I began to see how even the glamour of performing can become just a job. I wasn't unappreciative of responsive audiences or good critical reviews, but I knew my career with Ciro was illusive because of his age, our unprofessional lifestyle which gave priority to remodeling a house, grocery shopping, and generally making ourselves unavailable to more serious work. My heart wasn't in it; I had fallen in love with Il Poggetto and Aurelio, turning my ambition away from performing music for the first time in my life. But we still had contracts to fulfill, and In mid-October we gave another concert. It was in unusual circumstances that I didn't particularly like. We were engaged to play in a popular discotheque in Forte dei Marmi, a resort near Viareggio on the Tyrrhenian Sea. Naturally we weren't to perform with strobe lights on us while bodies undulated nearby. We were booked for Sunday night when the disco was closed and were scheduled to play at midnight for an invited audience. It was a publicity stunt for the discotheque; they wanted to upgrade their clientele. The regional TV station was going to tape us for broadcast, and we got good newspaper publicity both before and after the performance.

We arrived early on Saturday and checked into the hotel provided for us, just across the street from the club. We loved the accommodations as the hotel had been one of the elegant villas from an earlier time and still gave an air of gentility and graciousness. From our room we could see the marquee announcing our concert.

The club, located on the broad beach, was a new two-story building with enormous windows overlooking the sea. Downstairs was the main dance floor surrounded by tables and chairs. A restaurant and small dance floor were upstairs, where we would perform. Ordinarily there were a singer and pianist/accompanist who performed during dinner. A second grand piano was brought in for our use; the tables were moved out, and the seats – cushy armchairs – were lined up more or less as in a theater. There were a lot of blind spots behind pillars, and worst of all, the lighting was much too dark and moody, making it difficult for us to see the keyboards.

Before we could rehearse on Sunday afternoon, the slick, young, black-haired proprietor had to chase out about a dozen couples who had come to the downstairs "tea dance" and were in various stages of lovemaking on the lounge chairs. The lighting man arrived and worked a long time with us, but he wasn't able to give us suitable illumination on the keyboards. Finally someone brought in two supplementary lamps to be put on each piano.

The proprietor, Dino, energetic and smiling, did his best for us. After the rehearsal we had dinner at the club and enjoyed the excellent seafood available. Ciro ordered his favorite dish, *sogliola alla mugnaia* (sole sautéed in butter sauce), and I had *tonno alla griglia*. Fresh tuna steak is as akin to American canned tuna as a good plate of pasta is to Spaghettios – no comparison. During dinner Ciro behaved badly with the waiter, complaining about what he considered the slow service and the relatively loud music, but as always I bent over backwards to be congenial to balance his temperamental behavior.

On Sunday Ciro insisted that I go the beach and swim; ordinarily I love both activities, but I felt in a work mood and did not like the looks of the murky sea. Ciro prevailed, so to the beach we went, then lunch and a nap. On Sunday night we arrived at the club at 10:30. Before going on stage, like most artists Ciro and I prefer to remain alone to prepare psychologically, to warm up vocally, and to mentally rehearse rough spots. This particular evening several friends were in our dressing room. Thinking they were doing us a favor helping us pass the time, they came in to chat. Janet, the American who gave everyone the *tu*, came in with her nobleman husband and four guests. We didn't want to be rude and ask them to leave as they had come quite a distance to be with us and, of course, they were willing to go along with the late hour. Ciro and I carried on as if the others weren't in the room, talking over the program in detail. After a while, our friends realized that they were in the way and went out into the audience.

By 11:45 I was in a daze. I went against my Mediterranean diet and drank a Coke to perk me up. I needed to be sure to drink the carbonated syrup early enough before the performance so I wouldn't burp my way through "The Man I Love." Not surprisingly, we didn't go on until after 12:30, when the still smiling Dino determined that all his guests had arrived. We did a one-hour program without intermission. As long as the TV cameras were rolling, we had plenty of light, but once they crept away we could barely see our hands on the keys. The spotlights highlighted us but cast shadows on the pianos. At the end we received an engraved silver plaque from Dino, fabulous red roses for me, and an enthusiastic reception from the 150 jaded guests present. One of the women in the audience, Signora Simi, was an agent who was able to book us on national TV the following month. Even with our success, I was happy to return the club to its disco status and go back to the peace of the country.

16. . . . AND MORE

Signora Simi, the agent, arranged for us to play on Rai Uno, the major TV network. We were scheduled on a midday game show, a live transmission, that featured various actors and performers between one game and another. Since we knew a couple of weeks in advance that we were going to be on, I watched the program to become familiar with the hosts and the format. (Ciro wasn't even curious to see the transmission.) There were different mindless games, mostly with contestants phoning in, and with a few housewives participating in the studio. Some time was devoted to guests who were interviewed, then performed their specialty. We were told that we would have approximately 10 minutes in all, six minutes of interview and three to four minutes of duo-piano playing.

Ciro wrote a mini-arrangement of "An American in Paris" for the occasion; it seemed awfully short, but it covered the themes. We rehearsed long hours since the TV exposure was a tremendous opportunity for us as it was certain to lead to other engagements. All our expenses were paid by Rai, and we were to go a day ahead as we needed to be at the studio by 10:30 the morning of the show.

At the train station in Rome, we were met by our hostess, a girl of about nineteen who had just begun working at Rai. Her name was Elisabetta, and she knew of us from Richard and Kenneth, our friends with the car-eating ditch in their front field. Elisabetta came from their same hometown near Arezzo.

Outside Rome's *stazione* Termini a car was waiting with Elisabetta to take us to a hotel very near the TV studio complex. Elisabetta filled us in on various details during the ride: she and the driver would come for us at 10:00 the following morning. Once at Rai we would be introduced to our interviewer, given a dressing room, and taken down to makeup. We would be driven from the TV station to the Rome airport for our flight to Pisa, where we had another concert the following evening.

Rome was rainy, so we stayed in the hotel all evening. Besides, we were not there as tourists. At dinner Ciro ordered the wine displayed at our table – something he ordinarily would never have done because of the expense. He figured we could allow ourselves a little luxury as Rai was footing the bill. I took a look at the label; it was unknown to me. The red *vino nobile* was rich and fruity with 12.5 percent alcohol. Dinner was expensive but not memorable – our thoughts were on the following day's performance.

When I got up the next morning and looked in the mirror, I was horrified. The wine must have had some foreign chemical in it, for my face was bloated, and there were dark circles under my eyes. I had drunk very little, conscious of the following day's responsibility. I complained to Ciro, but he was too anxious about his performance to pay attention to my looks. I had experienced these same physical symptoms in the past with tainted wine. As we were to be in the TV studio for two and a half hours, I didn't dare start drinking a lot of water to rinse out the impurities, but that was the only cure I knew of.

At 10:00 sharp Elisabetta came for us; we were waiting in the lobby. She looked closely at me but didn't say anything. It was still raining, but it didn't matter, as we would re-dress at the studio. The Rai TV complex was in an enormous building with a formidable sculpture of a rearing horse in the front courtyard. Security was tight. We had to show our passports to uniformed guards on entering even though we were with Elisabetta. The security man checked his list and had us sign in. There was a crush of people coming to work at that hour, all behaving in true Italian style – no waiting in line, just shove and shout as you go.

Once inside we said goodbye to the world. We went through endless corridors and past many rooms – dressing rooms, studios, offices – with not a single window anywhere. Elisabetta showed us our dressing room; a gray, sparsely furnished cell. We dropped off our stage clothes, were given a key, and were told to keep the room locked at all times.

Next Elisabetta took us down to makeup. The hostess of the show, named Marchini, was already being worked on. Her dark curls shielded her big eyes as she studied her notes; "Oh, what you do is so interesting!" she said, then added, "We'll talk later." I thought she meant we would get acquainted before the show, but she intended, "See you on camera!"

We went on to the next room, to the men's hairdresser. "Can you quickly give me a head of hair?" Ciro asked half-seriously. We left him there and headed towards the women's hairdresser. In the hall the various dancers from the show, all young and thrilled with their jobs at Rai, were humming and practicing their routines. In their cowboy themed costumes of red and yellow vests with fringe and red cowboy hats, they were made-up and ready to go. Elisabetta left me with the hairdresser. The woman was my idea of a Roman: dark-haired, dark-eyed, with a sort of Mother Earth sexiness and plenty of self-assurance. She was good-natured and not easily excited, everything *pian piano*. She didn't do much with my hair, but when I said that it needed to be off my face for playing the piano, she pulled the sides back and fastened them with good old American bobby pins.

In makeup the woman had a fixation about lipstick. I had noticed it on various female guests on the shows I had watched from at home. These women all appeared on the air with vibrant red lipstick and an enlarged lower lip. Now I knew the source of this new style of lip cover. And once that lipstick was on, it was there to stay. So after her makeup, there I was with puffy cheeks, circles under my eyes, and enormous red lips, ready to be seen by six million people!

Back in the dressing room, Ciro and I dressed quickly. He didn't notice my appearance in particular, but he approved of my red silk dress and new black patent, very high heels. At least I was satisfied with the wardrobe department. The hairdresser hadn't been able to fulfill Ciro's wish for an instant head of hair, but he was always suave when he wanted to be.

A half-hour before the show began, we were taken to the studio. The frustrated piano tuner was struggling with our two pianos while the dancers from the hall filed in and began rehearsing their number to taped music. The leading lady Marchini was on stage singing and doing some kicks to celebrate having got her leg out of a cast the evening before. Everyone else was milling around, *espresso* in hand. Ciro and I both felt vaguely ill from nerves; waiting to go on is always nerve-wracking. Elisabetta checked on us constantly from our crowded off-stage waiting area. As we sat behind a heavy curtain on two straight-backed chairs, she brought us water and Kleenex and answered questions.

The set was a large stage with elaborate lighting where the pianos were, two sections where the game

140

boards were set up, a small area for a six-piece combo, and a living room for the interviews. We were to enter on camera from behind clouds that would separate like a curtain, do the interview, then play our mini "An American in Paris," after which would come a commercial break.

At 11:30 the program began. We watched it on a monitor in the cramped quarters backstage. At 12:23 the clouds parted for us. Meanwhile back at Il Poggetto, Nino gave a whoop, and the other workmen rushed to the TV set Nino had been watching since 11:30.

During the interview Ciro responded to Marchini's questions about his Florentine background, his family, and Gershwin. He was charming and came off very well. When he got to the "An American in Paris" story, I chimed in with my taxi horn beeps. In fact, I beeped several times as the first time I had come in wrong. The interview was over, and all I had said was "beep-beep-beep . . . bup-bup-bup."

The worst was yet to come; we still had to play the pianos. Before the program had started, I had said to Ciro, "There are several sets, so just follow me when we go from the interview to the pianos." "Yes, okay," he replied definitely. But when it came time to go to the pianos, he got lost. I arrived onstage thinking he was at my heels only to find myself alone on camera while he wandered around the studio. Finally after what seemed *un eternità* the producer got him in place and we began playing "An American in Paris." The pianos were horribly out of tune, though the tuner had done his best under the circumstances. About halfway into the number, those in the studio were given the sign to applaud. This was an idea some Italian TV producer had come up with, supposedly to show enthusiasm, but for the performer it was very distracting. In fact, Ciro took it as a cue to stop playing, thinking our time was up. When I kept going he came back in, and we finished the piece. Cut

141

to commercials. The producer rushed over and shook hands. He asked us to remain for the rest of the show. He was thrilled, Marchini was enthralled. We weren't so enthusiastic – no complacency here! – but they had given us twenty-four minutes rather than the ten we had been told.

Once we were off the air, we had little time to change clothes before our Rai driver, minus Elisabetta, came to take us to the airport. The flight to Pisa took about a half-hour during which my swollen face returned to normal. On arrival we were met by the sponsor's son, a 28-year-old architect named Michele. This time we were giving a private concert for a convention of heart surgeons from all over Italy. They were paying us our best fee yet, about $1,200.00, plus all expenses, and wavy-haired Michele served enthusiastically as our chauffeur and man Friday and couldn't do enough for us.

This concert was to be held in a jewel of a 17th century theater in the small town of Monte Carlo, not far from Pisa. The theater even had a raked stage, sloping towards the audience, the better to see the upstage actors. When we sat down to rehearse, we felt as though we were going to slide into the front row. The piano tuner propped up each downstage piano leg, and with some alterations to the benches we recovered our equilibrium.

Ciro got especially nervous the day of this concert, probably because we were being paid relatively well, and he felt under pressure more than usual to put on a good show. He looked pale and felt ill all day. At lunch he could barely eat anything, and dinner wouldn't be until after the performance and in the company of all the doctors. He never did get himself under control, and the concert didn't go well. That marked the beginning of the end of our duo-piano programs, for as much as Ciro didn't want to admit it, his playing was beginning to take its toll physically. Over 80 years old, he was still an extraordinary pianist, but his memory was unreliable and his fingers often didn't respond as he wanted.

Realizing that our concertizing was threatened left me with regrets. Ciro hadn't allowed me to perform with him in our early years together – he didn't want to share the stage – and now, just as we were having success, albeit limited, he couldn't take it physically. Adopting Il Poggetto in place of Palm Beach and concerts offered such an extreme that I couldn't even compare them, just as I couldn't compare Ciro with Aurelio. I was trying to cope with the emotional turmoil in my life by accepting a new role.

In late autumn we were engaged to play a concert on the coast of Spain in Marbella, near Malaga. Ciro's sister Beatrice, called Bice, had arranged it through the local Friends of Music. We were to arrive several days ahead of the concert and remain a few days after, making the expense-paid trip ten days in all. I looked forward to being in the sun, but would have preferred to return home sooner, not only because of my interests and passion for Tuscany but knowing my sister-in-law's manner and lifestyle.

Bice (pronounced Bee-che), a lithe, energetic octogenarian, enjoyed along with her ambassador husband a luxurious villa on the sea with mountains at its back. At one end of the long, bright living room there was a permanent raised platform for flamenco dancing, yet there was no piano in the house. We were given access to practice rooms for daily rehearsals at the local low-budget music school. To get to the practice rooms, we had to skirt behind the open fish market. Bice's house had servants, so I was able to relax without worrying about cooking, cleaning up (a major chore when Ciro cooked), or doing housework of any sort. I couldn't imagine two more different lifestyles than this one and the one I had adopted at Il Poggetto.

143

The Friends of Music was a group of mostly English expatriates. Their concert series had been in existence for over twenty years, and their guest artists had been among the musical elite. Placido Domingo served as honorary chairman. The sponsors here, too, were leery of a Gershwin program. Ciro decided to veer from all-Gershwin and composed a two-piano flamenco especially for this date. We practiced introducing all the numbers in both Spanish and English.

The concert was to be given in the ballroom of a large modern hotel on the outskirts of Marbella. A platform was built for the two pianos, and we were given good lighting and microphones. A platform can never substitute for a built-in stage, but we were accustomed to performing under less than ideal circumstances. Bice provided us with a hotel room for the day of the concert so we could rehearse, rest, and dress right there.

Though she meant it as a generous gift, the gown she gave me to wear was something I would never have chosen to perform in. It was a dress that had been made by the Sorelle Fontane, famous Roman couturieres, a number of years earlier, probably in the '60s. It was in perfect condition, but it had been created in the days when gowns had bones in the midriff. It was black lace, and I had always avoided wearing black on stage. Besides, I preferred to feel comfortable, not poured into a mold of bones. Nevertheless, I wouldn't have dared turn it down. The only time my sister-in-law paid attention to me was when she could give me something to wear; I didn't want to ruin our one meeting point.

The night of the concert there was an almost apocalyptic storm, but the tempest didn't deter the audience of 400 (the English, you know). Because of Bice's social contacts, there were various Spanish nobility, counts and countesses, ambassadors, and other VIPs, in the audience, and many new faces to the Friends of

144

Music. Our sponsors were impressed with the turnout and decided that Gershwin wasn't too profane after all – or if he was, it didn't matter. Ciro wasn't nervous for this concert, so his playing was up to par. At the reception after the concert, we were given truly gratifying compliments, but the press coverage in the following days was a big disappointment; it was clear that the woman who wrote us up had not been present at the concert and had used us to write a who-was-there society column based on secondhand information.

In the anticlimactic days following the concert, we toured nearby towns, window-shopped in boutiques geared to celebrities, and ate a lot of fish, bought at the entrance to the music conservatory. For me the days were interminable. Walking on the beach one cloudy day with Ciro and Bice, she gave Ciro a lecture which influenced me not so much because of its content but because of her tough attitude. She said, "I don't care what other people want; it's what I want. I go after what I want and make people do what I want." Her pep talk had no effect on Ciro, who had heard it all his life from his sister, but it found its mark on the wrong target and in the wrong way.

I was grateful that my character was not like hers. I knew women (and men), who reached their goals of money, fame, and power through conniving, intrigue, and hypocrisy. I neither admired nor wanted to emulate such people. Ciro's life had been dominated by these types, though he himself, being an artist, had escaped such self-aggrandizing. He had faults but was not false. He should have had such a person as his sister to manage his, then our, career, but he wasn't capable of working with such people. As his wife and collaborator, I offered help that was limited to the creative end. Because of these limitations, Bice didn't take me seriously and all but ignored me.

Moving to Il Poggetto meant escaping from what his sister had advised. My Tuscan home represented mental and physical well-being. In my new life, I was readjusting priorities, redefining friendships, and rediscovering goodness of heart and soul, *pian piano*.

17. WHERE THERE'S FIRE, THERE'S SMOKE

A few days after our return home, I thought it a good idea to test the new fireplace. Autumn temperatures inspired visions of sitting in front of a homey fire. I phoned Aurelio: "You are invited to the first lighting of a fire in the fireplace!" He arrived that evening, freshly shaven and smelling good. We recalled how a few months earlier the huge stone mantle had been placed on its side by Nino and how Aurelio had insisted that I order (in my meek way) that the stone be put upright, displaying its grandeur. So much had happened since that important occasion, and at last we were going to use the fireplace.

Ciro wanted to build the fire in his usual way, with mounds of crumpled newspaper placed under a pair of logs. Aurelio watched him and made faces at me. We felt like two teenagers in the parlor chaperoned by my elderly uncle. Aurelio managed secretly to take my hand several times, and I nearly exploded in laughter at the secret signs between us. This emotional immaturity, I recognized later, stemmed from neither of us having been allowed a normal childhood. Aurelio had begun working at 14, and I had spent my earliest years practicing the piano rather than playing games. We were making up for those lost days now.

As for the fire, it didn't catch. Ciro was all for adding more newspaper, but Aurelio calmly took over, building a fire with small sticks of kindling rather than paper. The flames grew higher, and a fine fire was burning brightly when suddenly to our horror the fireplace began sending clouds of smoke back into the room. If we opened the exterior door slightly, the smoke found its way up the chimney; otherwise the smoke billowed towards us. Ciro was furious at the shopkeeper who had sold us the guaranteed-not-to-smoke prefabricated fireplace. Aurelio, having had experience with the problem before, thought about how to fix it. He said, "This happens a lot here. We say, 'Leave the door open for the cat,' meaning the fireplace smokes." I was stunned. I couldn't believe this piece of bad luck was happening. The fireplace was the heart of my home.

The smoking fireplace brought various technicians and chimney "witches" to the house. The dealer who had sold us the unit took no responsibility, saying that the chimney had not been installed to specifications. Aurelio emphatically denied this accusation saying that every measurement had been followed exactly. In the end, general opinion was that the chimney needed to be higher, the better to draw the smoke.

Aurelio told me to order Gattone to send two workmen the following Monday morning to raise the chimney. I was still shy at insisting with Gattone, but, in fact, it worked. Aurelio and Fabio were on the job early Monday, compliments of Gattone. The chimney was raised about twelve inches. Holding our breaths we watched Aurelio light a small fire. The Tuscan pessimistic mentality influenced me to believe that the repair would not resolve the problem, but I hoped with all my heart that it would. Aurelio's face reflected confidence mixed with trepidation. He had confidence in his workmanship but knew so well that building quirks could cause imperfect results. The fireplace still smoked.

Several months later, undaunted Aurelio raised the chimney still more, working on a cold, windy day when a normal man wouldn't have dared go on a roof. I stayed on the ground and kept an eye on him, worried that he might slip on a roof tile and fall. The fireplace did not stop smoking. Rather than tolerate the smell, the grayed walls, and the teary eyes caused by smoke, we did not light the fireplace at all.

For heating and cooking I decided on liquid propane gas. Raffaella used oil in her home and urged me to do the same, but I didn't like the smell and the noise of the enormous furnace involved. Residents of the town had natural gas, but I was too far out to hook up so had no choice but to put in a *bombolone*, the large tank that would hold LP gas. The local gas company installed the tank in the only feasible spot, unfortunately right at the top of the driveway, about thirty feet from the house. If it had been put behind the house, it would have been visible from the music room and upstairs guest room. If placed on the far side of the house, the fuel truck would have had to pass over the future front terrace or back lawn to get to it. So there it stood, "white as milk" as Aurelio described it, fenced in and difficult to hide from arriving guests. I planted bay bushes around the fence hoping that they would grow quickly and as tall as some I had seen in town. Ciro shook his head: "Those will never grow."

In late autumn several *operai* had returned to Il Poggetto and the downstairs projects were underway. Nino whistled as he enlarged the windows in the former stall, and another man began putting in the wiring. Ciro still envisioned one end of the remodeled room as home to two grand pianos. I indicated wiring for overhead lights and marked the floor plan with plenty of outlets and two wall fixtures on opposite ends of the stall.

The steel-haired plumber, Paci, came to finish the downstairs bathroom, ex-pigsty. The fireproof exterior door was installed at the same time as the heating plant. The heat and hot water came from an amazing, quiet little wall box that was fed the liquid propane. The music-room windows would not be ready until March, so there was no point in painting that room yet. Even most of the baseboards (*battiscope* or "broom hitters") were already in place. Downstairs there would be no characteristic shutters because of the iron grillwork, but the upstairs shutters were ready to be painted and were stored in the carport until spring.

The house really began to take shape with the arrival of some furniture from the States. A few Italian antiques that Ciro had owned through the years were shipped back over to Tuscany from Florida. Ciro liked the idea that the large inlaid desk and handmade monks' chairs would be in their home country again and looked forward to their arrival.

At last the moving van with the container full of our goods arrived. But the enormous truck couldn't risk crossing the makeshift bridge over the stream between my house and the sharecropper's farm next door. No *operai* were on hand, and Ciro hid in the studio, not wanting to deal with this latest problem.

I made several desperate phone calls looking for a small truck that could haul the furniture the last 400 yards up to the house. Gianmarco was at the police station, but he had no helpful ideas; Gattone was unreachable. This time an Ape was too small and lightweight to do the job. Having no success, I went to Manlio's farm, the nearest to the bridge, and found a strong young workman there who had the ideal truck. He balked at the idea of helping me as it interfered with his current project at the farm.

At last I convinced him to give up a few minutes. The furniture was hurriedly carried in and left in the dining room to be placed appropriately when the rooms were ready.

The movers and the man with the truck all received a well-earned tip and went off to eat lunch. When Ciro emerged, the commotion had ended, and he was amazed and pleased to see his furniture back on its home soil.

18. *PASSERÀ ANCHE QUESTO*

Ciro and I had long-standing plans to return to the States in November. It would be our first trip back to Florida since arriving on April 2nd. We were going for only two weeks, so I decided to leave Puffi behind at Il Poggetto and in Aurelio's care. I was leaving my heart behind, as well.

The evening before our flight was drizzly and foggy. Aurelio came to get me at 5:30; it was already getting dark. "Where do you want to go?" he asked.

"The *pineta*," I answered without hesitation. We were both quiet as we drove up beyond town to the pine forest. It wasn't raining there, just misting, and it seemed less cold than at the house. He reclined both our seats. He was crying. This time it was my turn to comfort him after the many times he had comforted me. "I remember two or three months ago," I began, "when I was afraid of losing you. You said to me, 'You're too important to me. Even when I'm far away, I'm always with you.' Those words helped me a great deal. I'm yours; you are my soul mate, my *anima gemella*. As I have always told you, I didn't have any hopes of finding a man like you, and you've not disillusioned me for one instant. I love you with all my heart."

He remained quiet and made love to me tenderly, and we held each other close for a long time.

Early the following morning, Aurelio came to take u. to the train station in Chiusi. The weather was still gray and foggy. Ciro remained upstairs till the last minute, hectically gathering last-minute articles to carry along. I was already downstairs. Aurelio held me in his arms without saying a word. As he drove us to the station, tears rolled down his cheeks. Ciro, in the front seat beside him, didn't notice. I was too numb to cry. As the plane flew out of Rome, I tried to comfort myself with the familiar quote, "This too shall pass." Now in Italian translation it took on new meaning: *Passerà anche questa.*

The two weeks back in the States were a nightmare. Arriving at the house in Florida, I found everything as it had been left, and that gave me the feeling that I had never been to Sarteano, never seen Il Poggetto, except in a fantasy. Far from Ciro's earshot I phoned the house just to hear the telephone ring. I worked nonstop at the projects Ciro assigned me to help pass the time. There were lists of jobs to do: taxes to pay, attorneys to see, bankers to consult, the preparation of the Florida house in hopes of letting it, a new publicity brochure to write. We moved around, too. My sister-in-law Bice had returned to Connecticut from Marbella and wanted to "help" us professionally. Ciro always felt he was making headway if he looked up timeworn contacts in New York, so we traveled north from Florida by car. He was enthusiastically in his element.

Finally one of the many times I phoned Il Poggetto, Aurelio answered. "*Buon giorno, Signora!*" he cried. He and the other men were laying the tiles in the living room, (the former stable), and outside they were preparing to pave the stone walkway that was to go all around the house. I asked about Puffi. "She's fine. She eats everything; she's not afraid of getting fat!" he teased.

Then he lowered his voice: Have you found an Arab down there? A Bedouin?" "I have nothing but work here," I reassured him, "there's no chance of any Arab." Then he murmured one of his pet names for me, saying, "*Trottola,* I miss you." At the end of the conversation I told him to give Puffi a hug for me. "No, no, I'm not touching anybody; I'm all alone," he said.

I lived off our occasional phone conversations during those two weeks in Florida. Aurelio would always tease me about finding an Arab or Bedouin or even a cannibal who would steal me from him. I would laugh through my tears, and he would always make an effort to cheer me up, though he was suffering, too.

Finally November 23d arrived, and we were back in Rome. The plane had been three hours late getting in, so the earliest train we could catch wouldn't arrive in Chiusi until 8:00 that evening. Aurelio had told me to phone him at lunchtime and tell him our arrival time so that he could meet the train. Instead we were so late that he was already home for the day when I called. "I'll be right there!" he cried, and when the train pulled into the station, he was waiting on the chilly platform, his face flushed with anticipation. With the excuse of helping me off the train, I gave him my hand. Ciro had got off first, but Aurelio and I walked ahead with some of the bags, telling Ciro we would make two trips so that he wouldn't have to carry anything heavy. Outside the station I couldn't resist giving Aurelio a quick embrace, though it may have been indiscreet. I was home at last.

At the house, Puffi danced when she saw me. I found the garage had been re-roofed and new floor tiles laid, a wide travertine windowsill had been installed in the kitchen, and the upstairs floors were waxed and polished. Part of the outside walkway was done, and best of all, the heat was on. Aurelio had covered the music room window openings with heavy plastic to keep out the cold; Calvi was slow in making the windows with their grillwork. With the money I had left behind for expenses, Aurelio had bought a swivel TV stand and a small telephone table for the downstairs phone. He had planted two Golden Delicious apple trees.

It wasn't cold yet, but the wind was strong. The swallows had migrated south, and the tiny, rotund robins had replaced them. Everything was still green, and the olives were beginning to ripen on the trees. Ciro had felt stimulated in the US; back in Sarteano, immediately he sank into the doldrums. He moved both the twin beds from the master bedroom into the guest room, pushed them together, and slept there. I used a set of cheap mattresses on flimsy frames, but was so relieved not to share the room with him anymore that the discomfort didn't matter.

Aurelio and I resumed our almost daily encounters. Either he would come to Il Poggetto with the excuse of doing some work, or I would drive into town to meet him and we would go up to one of our many secret spots – places he knew as a hunter. Our outings were not sexual escapades for the most part. I was still in a lost-lamb syndrome. I clung to Aurelio, and any courage I could muster came from his strength and psychological support. My newfound feelings of security would disappear if I didn't see Aurelio for two days running. At that point I would begin having doubts about him, about Il Poggetto and the future.

As insecure as I was, though, Aurelio was equally afraid that I would find someone else, a *signore* who would steal me away. At times he would say, "When you decide to leave me for another, tell me early in the day, will you? Maybe that way I can cope a little better."

Ciro was still jealous, but was not suspicious that Aurelio was seducing me in the music room instead of hanging a light fixture. Sometimes Ciro would sneak up on us to see what we were doing, but we were too clever ever to be caught doing anything but our work. What should have given us away was my total unhappiness with Ciro. He recognized that, and became ill-tempered because he couldn't do anything about it. I was desperate as to what to do with Ciro. I knew we couldn't go on as we were, and yet I had bought this house primarily to please Ciro.

With winter's short, dreary days, I missed Aurelio's daily presence at Il Poggetto. Before he had been transferred to another job I had told him I didn't know how I could face the long days without him. "I'll come everyday to see you," he had said. "You're too important to me." He repeated what we had said to each other before: "I'll always be with you, even when I'm far away."

By 5:30 each dark afternoon I knew that Aurelio was off work, so I sat at the bedroom window pretending to write at my child-sized desk while staring down the driveway for his car. With only a single bare light bulb hanging from the ceiling, Ciro would appear long enough to chide, "Stop working there; it will ruin your eyes." When Aurelio turned into the long road up to the house, he would have only the parking lights of his Fiat on to keep from being noticed by inquisitive neighbors (especially Raffaella) or even by Ciro. His arrival each evening was the only important daily event, now that no workmen were on the job. Until I saw his car coming up the drive, I would think I couldn't cope with life any longer. Ciro had become a menacing shadow with never a kind word or look but always putting me to work on his writing projects. And now, added to his musical ones, he had decided to write a cookbook. Having seen no success in any of our writing endeavors, I was no longer interested in them. More and more I could see his shortcomings as a writer, and I realized that his ideas were not likely to be marketable. A talented writer in New York, a friend who had tried to help doctor one of our scripts, said of it, "It will be a miracle if you get this produced."

When concert agents showed interest in booking Ciro and me, I purposely would find an excuse not to accept the date or just wouldn't remind Ciro to get in contact with the agent. My nerves were out of control. Sometimes I would disco dance while mopping the floor, intentionally wearing myself out. My new Tuscan doctor, Dottor' Viganò, told me that I had a tendency toward anorexia. Mostly I felt too numb to do more than minimal tasks.

The peaceful moments with Aurelio served to keep me going. Aurelio represented the positives in my life, Ciro only the negatives. Ciro tried to bully me into drinking too much alcohol; Aurelio told me to stop drinking or I'd not see him anymore. Ciro wouldn't give me time to get cleaned up and change out of dirty jeans before going into town. Aurelio instead told me, "You are a *signora*; people look up to you, and you must live up to their respect."

My Methodist mores learned as a child had little to do with this culture. Here it was important to give a good impression in public by dressing and grooming carefully. I found myself a long way from the Florida habit of running to Publix in shorts and flip-flops. My manner had to be pleasant but serious, personable but concise, frugal but debt-free, and I had to look good. These characteristics reflected a person's respectability more than attending church or touting American-style morality. To Tuscans, more immoral than a mature love affair was hypocrisy. Instead of worrying that I might offend a man by resisting his advances, my role here demanded that I tell him firmly, "*Mani a posto!*" (keep your hands to yourself). The local priest don Paolo and the other clergy were the only ones to proselytize about the Church. Respectable individuals practiced their religion in private and allowed others to believe as they chose. In Tuscany I had the difficult choice of whether or not to personally accept and live by the local mores, mores that would not have been acceptable in the US. But regarding Aurelio and our love, I did accept them. *Pian piano* my healing process began. Working the land proved to be part of the cure.

On December first Aurelio arrived, a 12-foot ladder strapped to the roof of his car. He showed me a large burlap bag and an oval wicker basket with a long cord attached to it. It was time to pick the olives! The basket was to be worn around his waist while Aurelio stood on the ladder picking, then when the basket was full, the contents were to be emptied into the burlap bag. Once brimming with olives, the bag would be emptied on a cane mat on the music room floor, where air could circulate among the olives so they would not mildew.

Each olive was handpicked, and those on the ground were to be gathered as well. I was designated ground picker. I learned that my *oliveto* had three varieties of olives; the small, black *morellini*; the *coriggioli*, the variety that had the best yield; and the *orioli*, large and almost opaque. After watching Aurelio's technique I felt confident enough to pick during the day when he was at work, then he would arrive and climb to the highest limbs where he forbid me to go, afraid for my safety. Some days I couldn't work because it rained; the moisture would have damaged the small branches if picked when wet. In my enthusiasm I tasted a fresh-picked olive, but spit it out as soon as I realized how incredibly bitter it was!

Olive trees demand little care during the year, not nearly as much as regular fruit trees like pear or apple. They must be pruned in the spring, fertilized spring and fall, and be sprayed with copper fungicide for insects annually. An ongoing task is to keep the ground around each tree clean. That work is nothing compared with the constant attention a vineyard demands. Still, the fact the olives were picked in November or December meant at least a few days of numbed feet, daredevil limb-hanging while facing the northern *tramontana* wind, and bruised shins where the ladder was bound to hit. I wore heavy, fleece-lined boots, thick socks, long underwear, jeans, and several layers of sweaters and jackets. If the weather warmed up during the day, I could simply shed one or two garments.

If the olive yield was large enough, rather than the wicker basket, a huge net, like those fishermen use, was placed around the base of the tree, and as the olives were picked they were dropped into the net.

There are a lot of myths about olive oil: what makes it "virgin," how healthful the oil is, and whether or not cold pressing is important. The truth is straightforward: extra virgin oil is pure olive juice. To be considered extra virgin, it must have less than one percent acidity. At the mill the olives are rinsed with cold water and sent through a separator that picks out the debris; then, the olives are squashed, pits and all, under a rotating millstone. The result is virgin olive oil. Most people confuse virgin oil with sexual virginity, thinking that to be virgin it has to come from the first pressing. Usually there is only one pressing. Another oil, called *sansa*, is made from the residue of the first pressing. For *sansa*, the pulp, already mashed fine, is milled further in a process that mixes it with hot water to get a bit more yield out of the olives. This oil is not virgin – not because it came from a later pressing, but because it is too acid to be classified as virgin. The olives, and later the oil, must not be heated during the first pressing, and the oil should not be strained or, of course, mixed with any other oil, a practice where the biggest commercial chicanery comes into play.

An acquaintance of mine, a German aristocrat who had lived in Tuscany for over thirty years, had trees that produced 500,000 liters of oil annually, so clearly he took an interest in the product. He sent samples of all the major brands of Italian extra virgin olive oil to be analyzed in a lab in Siena. Not one sample was pure. Any oil, even that for lamps, could be refined so that it was tasteless and odorless. When this product is mixed with olive oil, the consumer cannot tell the difference. Ordinarily the extra virgin olive oil is cut, sometimes with sunflower oil – oh! those charming fields of summer sunflowers in Italy! – or with an inferior quality oil from another country. The only way to be sure of getting 100 percent pure Tuscan virgin olive oil was to buy from a local producer you knew and trusted.

Tuscan *bruschetta* is a good way to judge the olive oil. It is simply lightly toasted bread rubbed with garlic and doused generously with olive oil, a sprinkling of salt recommended but optional. When my olive oil arrived from the mill, Aurelio and I made *bruschetta* for everyone who had helped pick the olives. There was Aurelio, of course, as well as his son and Nuccio. We all praised its flavor and celebrated the completed harvest. My first year's oil gave me a thrill, no matter how small the small yield. My olives had been combined with Nuccio's since I didn't have enough to merit their own pressing. The forty-seven kilos of olives from Il Poggetto yielded six liters of oil. To me it was liquid gold.

The weather turned colder, and the wind chilled us to the bone. Ciro asked Aurelio, "Does it get colder than this?" Aurelio answered, "This is candy!" It was only December.

Progress was not necessarily considered a good thing by the Sarteanans. Nothing worked better than the old-style wood stoves in the kitchen in winter, and food cooked in them was much tastier, with an authentic flavor not found in foods cooked in modern stoves. After suffering the cold my first winter in Tuscany, I got a wood

161

stove, a *cucina economica*. With over thirty large oak trees on my property and small ones growing all the time, I certainly had a supply of firewood, so the stove saved me from chilblains and maybe even pneumonia. When the upstairs was 54 degrees, downstairs with the stove blazing the temperature rose to 65 degrees. To turn up the gas that heated the radiators would have meant paying $400.00 a month for fuel; I preferred to stoke the stove.

19. CHRISTMAS HOLIDAYS

"*Natale con i tuoi, Pasqua con chi vuoi*" "Spend Christmas with your family, Easter with whomever you want"

For Christmas, Ciro and I bought a small, living tree and four colorful balls to hang on it. I put it upstairs by the fireplace and decorated it with the ornaments plus several pairs of the largest earrings I owned and a huge red bow instead of a star on top. Ciro was miserable spending Christmas at Il Poggetto. He missed the mild Florida climate and felt far from friends and relatives with nothing but fog and cold, damp weather, and me to keep him company. As a gift I gave him a food processor; he had complained about not having one, but he was not in the spirit. He had always loved getting me endless trifles to open as presents: inexpensive jewelry, jokes, personalized stationery, socks, and perfume. But he could no longer consider me that unsophisticated "girl," as he always called women. His childlike nature of fantasy and fun no longer had a playmate in me, and he resented it. I was, nevertheless, determined not to be held back any more.

On Christmas Day, Marisa, the friend who had driven us to Sorrento, and her companion of many years, Marco, came to lunch and brightened our holiday considerably. We exchanged gifts and ate a leisurely lunch. At about 3:30 Aurelio came up the driveway, but he didn't come in as he saw that we had guests. I went out and invited him to join us, but he was too shy. When Marisa asked about him, Ciro and I told her how generous he had been with his time, work, and help. She understood him immediately. "He's someone," she observed, "who is used to sacrificing himself; it is his way of life."

After our guests had gone, Aurelio returned to wish us *buon Natale*. I asked him to come in to see the tree. Ciro was pleased when he made much over it. We didn't dare build a fire in the fireplace for Christmas because of the as-yet unresolved smoke problem. New Year's Eve, though, the south wind, the *scirocco*, was such that we could have a fire without its sending smoke back into the den. At last the upstairs felt cozy with the cushioned armchairs, the fire, and the starry night outside the window. Having only an exterior staircase precluded winter breakfast in robe and slippers or a cup of tea in bed. I had to dress fully, including wearing a coat and hat, before going from one floor to the other. Sometimes the brick stairs had a thin, invisible layer of ice. Once, dressed up to go to Rome, I slipped and landed on the bottom two steps. Aurelio saw me fall, cried, "Ohhhh!" and was picking me up before I realized what had happened.

Early New Year's Eve I sat before the fire writing in my diary. I wrote of how my life had changed so drastically and unexpectedly since coming to Sarteano on April 2nd. I wished only that the New Year not bring too many more changes. At that point I hadn't the courage to separate from Ciro completely – he had played such an influential role in my life for over fifteen years. But I wrote in the diary that I would do anything to keep Aurelio, ". . . the man I had lost any hope of finding." Besides Aurelio there had been the events of rebuilding the house, as well as successful concerts. I realized that success was subjective, while artistry was a goal that would always be part of my life.

My health was coming back. I had given up hard liquor altogether and drank much less wine. I had seen what a false lift coffee gave me; and though I loved a cappuccino, coffee was mostly out of my life. My nerves were still in pieces, but that was understandable considering my lifestyle. But all in all, I was a new person in a new home with everything good to look forward to.

Ciro loved festivities, so despite his general mood, he wanted to celebrate the arrival of the New Year with a special dinner, starting with hors d'oeuvres and French 75s (champagne and brandy). My drinks ended up in a vase conveniently placed on the new dining room table (the gift from the town). For dinner we prepared what turned out to be a tough, bony leg of lamb. We thought the butcher had gypped us, and I swore that I would never return to that grocery store, but in our ignorance the choice of lamb at all had been a mistake: it was out of season. We had special wines, some of which I tasted, then finally Ciro polished off an after-dinner liqueur. After drinking so much, he got sleepy, and by 11:30 he had gone to bed and immediately to sleep.

I watched the New Year's festivities (an American gospel choir) on TV. Aurelio arrived a little after midnight, and we began the New Year, 1989, together. At midnight there were fireworks displays across the hills, some pyrotechnics being sponsored by the villages, others offered by locals who risked mutilated fingers or temporary blindness for their imprudent celebrating. But for those of us who simply stood in the clear, frozen air watching the fireworks, it was a superb show along the entire horizon, something like a Tuscan aurora borealis.

On my first New Year's Day at Il Poggetto, I spoke to Aurelio by phone: *"Auguri*, Happy New Year!" he said, then added, "My mother is in the kitchen doing this year's weather predictions." He explained this tradition. His mother took the outer dry skins from several onions, each skin representing a particular month of the year. They were sprinkled with salt then thrown onto the hot wood stove. Those skins that "cried" meant a wet month, while those that shriveled up represented a dry month. I didn't know whether or not the women who did these predictions got together afterwards to compare notes, but there was bound to be a certain amount of accuracy by chance.

For those wanting more precise weather predictions, there was another tradition. The first twelve days of January correlated with the twelve months of the year. January 2 was February, January 3 was March, and so on. The actual weather on those first twelve days of the New Year indicated what the weather would be in the correlating months. If January 8 were cold and rainy, then August would be cold and rainy, despite that it was usually hot and dry. If this was not satisfactory enough as a prediction, the process could be done in reverse from January 13th back, thus getting a second version of how the weather would be during the year. No one actually believed in these predictions any more, but the tradition and ritual made them fun.

The holidays didn't end with New Year's Day. Epiphany, January 6, is an Italian national holiday. According to the Roman Catholic Church, it took the Wise Men following the star in the East until January 6 to reach Jesus' birthplace. For modern-day Italians of all ages, January 6 brings Befana, a kindly but very ugly old hag who, the night of January 5, leaves gifts as a reminder that every child could behave at least a little better.

Traditionally Befana originated as the ugly daughter of one of the three Wise Men. Her name evolved out of Epifania (Epiphany), a concoction easily understood considering how carelessly many Italians spoke. Befana is depicted in a cotton print skirt, long-sleeved shirt, apron, and with a head kerchief. She is required to have lots of warts and moles and a huge nose, and the uglier her other features, the better.

Santa Claus (Babbo Natale) existed too, having been imported from Germany under Mussolini's dictatorship. But Befana had been an Italian tradition for centuries and was nearer the hearts of the people. Naturally she did not need a team of reindeer, as she simply whisked around on her broom.

20. FIGHT TO THE FINISH

Early January brought new events. Gattone still was the workmen's boss, but from the period in which he had gone bankrupt (and put everything he had in his wife's name,) he had worked under another contractor. Aurelio came to the house with the news that Gattone had been fired from the company, and that he in turn had fired Aurelio's assistant Nuccio. All this happened just as I was about to finish up accounts with Gattone. We had to take the measurements of the house and compare them with those taken by Gattone: all figures had to be checked and double-checked and each bill gone over in detail. Geometra Landi was to review all the estimates Gattone had written up for the work on the house. Aurelio asked another *geometra* to measure inside and out just to be sure of all the figures.

In mid-January came the first one-on-one encounter between Aurelio and Gattone. Both men were at my house. I witnessed the meeting but didn't speak. Standing in the kitchen, they began arguing the minute Gattone arrived. The argument centered on Gattone's work shortcuts: the padded measurements of the walls, the empty beams over the doors, the fireplace

169

that smoked, the cheap tiles that Gattone had insisted I buy for the upstairs. But there was another point that I had not known about. According to law, the builder was required to put reinforced concrete in each reconstructed wall. Just like the reinforced overhead doorframes, this was a safety measure in case of earthquake. All along the north end of the house, Gattone had ordered the men not to use this reinforcement. That meant that there was a real danger of my bedroom wall collapsing.

But the two men didn't argue only about work. They attacked each other personally, and the bitterness Aurelio felt for this man came out through his anger. "You should be in jail for having cheated us out of our pension money," Aurelio pointed his finger at Gattone. Gattone's lack of scruples took over: "You guys don't matter to me; you're all good-for-nothings. Your children hate you because you've always neglected them." Aurelio: "I can walk with my head up anywhere; my children adore me. How dare you bring them up! Your wife and mother-in-law moved out when you told them all women are whores." "What's wrong with saying that?" Gattone turned and asked me with false ingenuousness. I stood mute, afraid they would have a fistfight then and there. Gattone told Aurelio not to come to work the next day and that if he did show up, Gattone would be waiting for him with a club. Aurelio laughed in his face, saying that Gattone didn't have the authority to fire him, which was true.

After two hours of detailed accusations, shouting and cursing, Gattone took his final bill, which he had expected me to pay right away, and drove off. Aurelio told me to go to Geometra Landi at 7:30 the following morning, before Gattone could get there first. "It will be hard for me to explain everything, but I'll do my best," I said. "Don't worry," he assured me, "I won't leave you to do this alone; I'll be there too."

The next morning I was explaining as well as I could to Landi the problems with Gattone. Aurelio arrived and filled in the details. Landi said not to sign anything and not to pay a single *lira* until everything was confirmed by his office. Later that day his partner came to Il Poggetto, and he, too, took all the measurements.

At 6:30 that evening, Gattone showed up with his little boy. The son was a shield in case Aurelio was there with me, as Gattone knew that Aurelio wouldn't cause a scene in front of the child. I told Gattone firmly and quietly that I would not sign any promissory note, nor would I give him a check, just as Landi had instructed me. Gattone tried to bully me. "You're just doing what Aurelio tells you – he doesn't know everything," he smirked. But I held out.

Then, since Aurelio was not present, he began gossiping about Aurelio and his family, as if I would believe a word of what he was saying. He claimed, for instance, that Aurelio's daughter was a drug addict, her arms full of needle scars and puncture wounds from shooting up. Gattone said things that he would not have dared to say in front of Aurelio because they were all lies. Unlike Tuscans, I couldn't be provoked by Gattone, ending the conversation with, "Well, you're wasting your time; I'm not paying now." I remained a *signora*. I got rid of Gattone for the moment, but he was back the next morning.

The final payment to the construction company where Gattone was associated was made via a promissory note, but I did not give it to Gattone himself. I went directly to the contractor and dealt with him. After all had been cleared by Geometra Landi, Aurelio helped us settle on a final sum that satisfied everyone. The shortcuts were not repaired, but sums were subtracted from the total for the work not done properly. I was reassured that the collapse of the wall was neither imminent nor even probable. (Even so, I quietly took out a hefty house insurance policy.) The promissory note was not due until spring, making it one full year in which I had dealt with Gattone. It had taken one year to accomplish what had been estimated as two months' work, and the house still was not finished. Total cost: $80,000. I felt satisfied that the contracted work was completed at last and considered the lowered final payment a triumph. Standing outside and looking at the house I was most impressed with its solidity. Like a small but mighty fortress, it dominated the property of Il Poggetto and on down into the valley. I couldn't believe all this was mine, every stone, each window. All the details were coming together at last.

Next I had to deal with the electric company. Gattone's construction company had tapped electric current furnished by what was considered a temporary line. After he and his men left the job, I continued to use that line, but transferred the account to my name. The temporary line meant power shortages and blinking lights. Aurelio prepared in the north exterior wall of the house a niche where the new meter was to be installed.

Finally an administrator from the electric company monopoly Enel arrived from Chianciano to survey my situation. A new line would be brought in and would cross underground in the field in front of the house. The meter would have to be placed at the bottom of the driveway, he said, since I chained off the road every night. We were not to risk having the meter reader locked out. At the site of the new meter would be the main current switch as well, a switch that was well known for shorting out during electric storms. That meant that I would have to put on boots and raincoat and trudge down the driveway at any hour of the day or night to turn the current back on.

"It is against the law to put the meter and switch in the niche you prepared," said the administrator. "But the electric company told me to build the niche there," I answered. "The laws have changed recently," he assure me. But I knew Raffaella was joining the new line, too, and that her meter was going to be installed under her carport, despite the enormous locked gates at the entrance to her property. When I told the company representative, he said, "Ah, but I have known that *signora* for many years." I argued, pleaded, and even got the man's superior to come and look over the situation. "We'll put a pole here near this tree," decided the superior. "Near the walnut tree?" I tried to confirm. "That's not a walnut tree," said the superior. "Strange," I couldn't resist correcting him; "it has walnuts every year" The superior was miffed; I guessed I could forget the niche now.

In the end the meter was installed not in the niche and not at the bottom of the drive, but at the top, near the house, and I promised (with my fingers crossed behind my back) that I wouldn't close off the drive any more. Rather than have a large concrete enclosure built to the specifications of the electric company, Aurelio erected a Madonnina to house the meter. It was a brick temple five feet tall and with a tile roof that matched the one on the house. Such small shrines to the Madonna grace roadsides all over Italy. Instead of a statue of the Madonna, mine has a metal door that encloses the meter and switch box. The vineyard next door copied my idea, and now others have caught on to the "electric" Madonnina.

With my new line came a new account, and I discovered that I had been paying the "non-resident" – rather than the much lower "resident" – rate for electricity. I went by myself to the regional office in Montepulciano. The clerks were all men. The one who waited on me was courteous and helpful, but he said that I would have to return when I had procured an official residence document from Sarteano's City Hall. At the office of statistics, gruff Felice told me that not only had I been considered a resident from the date of application the previous year but as Italian-born Ciro's wife I had been given citizenship as well. Without pledging allegiance to the Republic of Italy or even requesting it, I was an Italian citizen. Nothing could have pleased me more than having dual citizenship, as it made me feel that I belonged to Il Poggetto as much as it belonged to me.

Calvi delivered the music room's iron window frames at last, finishing up the work to be done by outside contractors. He had coated the frames with bright orange anti-rust paint, so I covered them with the green paint I had chosen for them, having disregarded Raffaella's insistence on unappetizing brown. The glass man brought the double-paned windows, and the music room was finally enclosed.

With the windows installed, I painted the music room walls with three coats of white paint as in the other downstairs rooms. On two of the walls, Aurelio mounted light fixtures I had bought months earlier. With a final floor washing, the last room to be finished was ready for its furniture.

The music room, lacking the dreamed-of grand pianos, became the formal and rarely used dining room, with the town's dining room table settled at the end of the room near the kitchen door. What had been planned as the dining room, with its archway and bar leading into the kitchen, instead became a cozy living room.

One afternoon during this period, Ciro and I were rehearsing with Aurelio came in. What was he doing at the house in the middle of the workday? He was limping. He had fallen from some scaffolding at work and needed to get his leg x-rayed. He came to me to take him to the hospital in Chiusi, using the excuse that all his friends were at work and I was the only person who was available to accompany him. We went in his car. It was his left knee that hurt him, but he was able to drive. At the hospital we waited for the results of the x-rays. He was actually in a good mood, joking with the other patients and with me, as always. The x-rays showed knee damage that required his entire leg to be put in a cast. I waited while it was encased, and when he reappeared the cast was still hot. He put his arm around my shoulders for support as we walked out to the car. I had to convince him to let me drive. I didn't realize what this accident would mean to him and to us, except I knew that at last he would get a well-earned rest.

Now Aurelio was free all day. All he had to do was give me a phone call, and I would go and pick him up near his house. When he would phone me he was always too shy to ask me directly to come and get him. He would say, "Are you coming into town today?"

By his second day at home, he was going crazy from boredom. He couldn't work, but he couldn't stay still. This was our chance to be together nearly everyday, away from everyone else. We would drive into the hills. When his leg wasn't bothering him, we would take a walk. If he was in pain, we would sit in the car and talk; often the conversation had to do with the house. One day he said to me, "I'm proud of you; you have become a woman, a real *signora*. When you first came here you were a little bird; now you're an adult." It was true. At last I was beginning to feel in charge of my own life and responsible for myself. Thanks to Aurelio and to the growth process that coming to Sarteano had given me, I was beginning to accept life as an independent and mature person. I relied too much on Aurelio and was still emotionally insecure, but just as he would not need his crutch for long, I knew the day would come when I would no longer emotionally lean on him.

After only two weeks, Aurelio's cast was removed. His leg was stiff, and his knee more painful without the cast. He walked with a cane, but little by little his exercises loosened up the muscles. Our daily encounters

175

continued, as he certainly was not in shape to return to work.

Early in February Ciro had one of his fits: he chastised me and generally ran me down for our unhappy marriage. "Why don't you sell this place? It is keeping me from doing what I want to do. We're not getting any dates, and I can't sell my shows or my cookbook from here. I am wasting my time and don't have that much left!" "But you wanted me to buy here, " I reminded him. "Yes, but not to live in except summers," he answered. "The people here are hicks; I can't deal with them. You shouldn't take them so seriously. You let them boss you around and make a fool of yourself. I gave you a life in Florida and introduced you to all my wealthy and influential friends, and now we're here. I'm above this sort of life; you have dragged me down to this. What would my sisters Gina or Bice say if they saw how we are living? You don't understand how important I am . . . I want out. You owe me for all I've done for you. You're Little Miss Nobody."

If I had been Ciro's sister Gina, I would have responded, "Don't be ridiculous. If it weren't for me you'd be nothing but a broken down pianist living off someone else. You can't write lyrics, you can barely rhyme "you" and "blue". I have given you a whole new career and my talents, not to mention the best years of my life. I have gone along with everything you wanted to do and have nothing to show for it. At least here I have the security of a home!" But not being Gina, I said nothing and simply fell further into Aurelio's arms.

Afterwards Ciro repented, as always, but it was too late. He felt better for having spouted off, but he had resolved nothing. He didn't refer to Aurelio at all; he believed that I was still living the life of a devoted nun. He thought that my unhappiness was all due to Il Poggetto's not being finished. He was unhappy at spending the

176

winter in Italy instead of in Florida and at being so far from the New York action. He wanted to get a tan and see his friends. We made plans to fly to Florida on February 16. I had in mind to stay there only three weeks, but I didn't tell Ciro. I wanted to be back at home for my birthday in March. Aurelio said, "*Cara*, you go stay with your mother where it's warm. Come back here in June when the roses are in bloom. '*Rose rosse per te . . .* ,'" he sang. But when I told him that I would be gone for only three weeks, he was relieved.

So on February 16, Aurelio again took Ciro and me to the train station. There were no tears this time, but oh! how I hated to leave. The States represented my past and offered only problems.

Ciro and I knew that we had to move out of our Florida house, but we didn't expect to have to vacate until May. Still, I packed as many things as we could spare and put the boxes out of the way in the guest room. There were hundreds of books, bric-a-brac, and miscellaneous treasures of Ciro's with which he had been unwilling to part through the years. Every time we had moved he had said, "Let's move everything, then when we get to the new house I'll go through it all and get rid of a lot." Instead, I was packing the things for the fifth time in nine years. The first and most complicated move had been when he sold his villa on the Tyrrhenian Sea. Then I had taken a studio apartment in Manhattan, and he decided he wanted to move with me into a one-bedroom in the same building. A year later, sick of the cold, we moved to a Spanish-style stucco home in West Palm Beach, then later built his dream house further up the Florida coast, the house I was packing up now. The charming family pieces – his mother's glued milk pitcher, his grandfather's deteriorating music volumes, a Sicilian silk shawl that mice had chewed on – these and endless items were to be kept. They had thrilled me in the early years when they were new to me; now they were worn relics of a

177

lost time, a life that Ciro clung to and I was burdened with.

When my three weeks in the States were near an end, I told Ciro that I was returning to Il Poggetto. He said simply that he would remain in Florida. We didn't talk about a separation, but neither did we make future plans. Despite Ciro's idealistic reminiscences of his childhood in Florence, he had been a patriotic American for decades. When it came down to it, the USA was where he wanted to live.

Ciro donned a camel hair sport coat to accompany me to the airport. I wore a conservative dressy suit, left over from my New York Republican Women's Club lunch days. Ciro looked large suddenly. Before leaving him behind, I searched his eyes for some redeeming sparkle of caring, but nothing came back to me. I walked away from him and felt immense relief, warm anticipation, and a little fear. I was afraid of being alone, but I knew at the end of this trip Aurelio would be waiting for me, face flushed, at the train station.

As the train pulled into Chiusi, I was excited for the first time in a long while. In earlier days excitement meant meeting Donald Trump, attending a White House reception or dancing to the society beat at Palm Beach's Red Cross Ball. When Aurelio and I saw each other, we felt pure joy. Back at Il Poggetto, we walked the fields arm in arm and with Puffi running alongside. Aurelio showed me all the work he had done in my absence: the trimming of the trees, cutting back of brush, feeding of the *oliveto*: also, he had finished up some details inside the house. All projects were accomplished despite the pain in his stiff leg. Il Poggetto was ours, I had told him. All his sacrifices were an investment. To him, though, the sacrifices were made for me, not the property. He was not interested in Il Poggetto without its *signora*, and I was not interested in it without Aurelio.

The first few nights alone were frightening, despite that Puffi kept me company. The total quiet kept us on

178

alert more than if there had been noises. A dog barking in the distance or the *chiù*, the horned owl's cry, were welcomed relief from the somber night. Aurelio repeated, "Even when I'm far away I'm still with you," gave me comfort, and I did not resent his not being with me. I knew that I would be physically alone every night from now on. When at last summer came, the nightingale's optimistic, constantly changing song lifted my heart, and I thanked God that I was in heaven at that moment to hear her sublime lullaby.

21. THE COMPLETE HELPER

I realized I couldn't handle my property alone. Aurelio took over as my *amministratore* gratis – gratis because of our relationship, but also because I didn't have the money to pay him.

For several years Ciro had been receiving money from a trust, and we lived like millionaires without any capital as a base. Just as I finished spending all my savings on Il Poggetto, the trust stopped making payments. My problems with Ciro had reached a head, and neither of us had enough income to live on.

Aurelio said that it didn't matter. When he first knew me, he had considered me pitiful. He had seen how both Ciro and Raffaella treated me, how they pushed me around, and how my self-esteem had been reduced to zero. In the early months at "Il Poggetto", I had walked with my head bowed and spoke in monosyllables, afraid of causing a confrontation with Ciro. "You were a little bird," recalled Aurelio. "You were a slave to your husband, and it was killing you."

So the lack of funds was nothing in comparison to regaining my physical and emotional well-being. Aurelio took over where I was incapable of running Il Poggetto.

If he didn't do a job himself, he arranged for the right man to do it: Nuccio to trim the olive trees, Marino to deliver gravel for the driveway, Bandelli to cut the fields. Aurelio teased a lot, but he wasn't a great conversationalist. When I asked him about his children's work or how his parents were, he would say, "You take care of yourself, don't worry about them." With outsiders he was a practitioner of *fai la tua* (mind your own business). As he gained confidence with me, though, he became my counselor in every aspect of life.

In Sarteano any young woman seen talking twice in public to a man other than her husband or close relative invited gossip. It might have been thought that I was involved with Gianmarco the policeman or even Don Paolo, who had a scabrous reputation, but even malicious gossips could not have found enough fuel to ignite much interest in my love life. Aurelio and I couldn't have been more discreet; we were never seen in town together except for the first time in the Ape, before people recognized me.

Aurelio's wife had told me once on the phone that he did not confide in anyone. Little by little he opened up to me, telling me about his past, and most of all talking about all he hoped to accomplish at Il Poggetto. When an unusual event took place, like the first day of hunting season, afterwards he would rush to tell me about it like a schoolboy running home to tell what had happened that day at school.

Though a mason by profession, Aurelio had grown up on a farm. He knew when and how to plant, fertilize, spray, repair implements, raise animals and then slaughter them. "I can do anything but give birth," he boasted, and then laughed.

Aurelio never interrupted me when I was practicing the piano. He said, "You were born to play the piano," and didn't want me to give it up. He took on the responsibility of the property with pleasure and pride. I gave him a free hand to do as he saw fit outside the house, and he left up to me the inside of the house. Even when he spent the entire day with me, he would go home for lunch. "They'll come looking for me if I don't show up at mealtime," he explained. I had brought him cologne once and a pair of Levi's another time from the States, but he wouldn't accept them. That was part of our work relationship.

There were times aside from work, though, when we would take day trips to Siena or Arezzo, eat in restaurants, or go to a neighboring town for a *gelato*. He always dressed well for these outings and expected me to live up to my role as *signora*. If a stranger happened to refer to him as my husband, Aurelio would say afterwards, "You were so proud you were about to burst." I knew he felt that way about me.

Along the road during these outings, he would point out the farms he had known as a boy, call my attention to a well-camouflaged pheasant in a field, or show me a hillside full of *sulla*, a wildflower with small red blossoms. If there were a patch of wild tulips or an abandoned rose hedge in bloom, he would stop the car and pick an enormous bouquet of the flowers for me. "This way you'll have something at home to remind you of me while I'm at work," he would say.

Always he would tease me unmercifully. He enjoyed making fun of my Italian pronunciation (I had trouble rolling my R's). I asked seriously if I were really so hopeless in the language. "If you were," he said, "I wouldn't tease you about it." He had endless pet names for me. Most often I was "*Trottola*," the word for a spinning top, here meaning a busy person. He called me "*gioia*," (joy) "*dolce*," (sweet) and "*cara*" (dear) with conviction, almost shouting them rather than murmuring these endearments. Sometimes he could call me by a name I did not recognize. I would ask, "What does it mean?"

and he would reply, "Ah, it's too beautiful, I can't tell you. You look it up in the dictionary." As soon as he had gone, I would look up the term: "*bolsa*" (wheezing horse) or "*bardassa*," (ill-mannered child). Once when I complained to him that while combing my hair that morning I found a gray one, he laughed. "There, you see? I'm not the only one getting older!" he joked. Ciro had always said that the best way to learn a foreign language was to have a lover who spoke that language and none other. Aurelio's English vocabulary was made up of two words: "jackass", which he had learned from a fellow mason in Switzerland, and "babysitter', from a lyric in a popular Italian song. After a while he learned, "Thank you very much," and would break into a big smile when he said it.

Not every moment was lighthearted. Some tiny mice were living in the carport. To me they were sweet; and when while working outside I would run across a little twitching nose, shiny black eyes, and tender pink ears, I wouldn't recoil in horror, but would smile and greet the creature with "Ciao." The reality, though, was that if the mice got in the house, I'd have trouble getting rid of them. I certainly didn't want them riffling through the muesli or leaving floury paw prints on the counter top.

Aurelio set a trap, and within a few minutes we heard it spring. A mouse was caught but not dead. I began to cry: "Please kill it; it is suffering!" Aurelio, impatient with my compassion for the rodent, said, "I suffer, too!" That gave me a good lesson in misspent tears. From then on I understood how one may have affection and respect for animals, but realized that they come second to humans. Ciro had influenced me with his storybook ideas of animals, but Aurelio taught me the reality of survival of the fittest.

It had been Ciro's childlike attitude towards animals and nature in general that had been my major influence up to that point. Once he was no longer in residence, I began living more like a *contadina*, learning the ways of the country. When I had bought Il Poggetto, Ciro's enthusiasm for the myriad blackberry bushes and for the *oliveto* rubbed off on me. Later I cursed the prickly bushes for their rampant, aggressive growth and earned every drop of olive oil in the work I did caring for the trees and picking the olives. Ciro had wanted to plant regal Tuscan cypresses up the driveway; Aurelio said that those trees represented a cemetery. Better to plant fruit trees, which would help nourish me. I felt pulled in two directions by this dichotomy of attitudes, but chose the Tuscan country way of life, alienating myself all the more from Ciro.

Being an outsider, especially an American outsider, and *bellina*, I was the perfect target for men looking for an *avventura*. The offers were somewhat scarce for at least two reasons: first was my husband's dominance in the beginning and second was because I was considered a "lady," the type of *signora* who did not let herself become involved in amorous adventures. Women by the hundreds from all social levels come to Italy to enjoy the charms of a Latin lover, but I was not considered in that category of female – not that I was supposed to be incapable or intolerant of sexual activity, but that I was discreet and highly selective.

The local men had a certain conceit about their charms with women. Even a toothless old coot thought he was a temptation. Gianmarco didn't understand why I had continued to turn him down, for he had been one of the first local men I had met. The fact that I might have preferred the second or twentieth man I'd met did not occur to him as a possibility, nor did it seem plausible that I may have preferred someone younger, handsomer, or more intellectual. Richer, yes, that was about the only competition to which the local men admitted defeat. I believe that this super-conceit came from the men's mothers who made them feel special, unique, of inestimable value. If a woman turned down a man's amorous advances, it was out of coyness, not because the man was unacceptable. When I spoke to Aurelio about a workman whom I thought had particularly good manners, Aurelio said, "First come the nice manners; then the man comes after you."

One chubby, baby-faced *contadino* farmhand came around two or three times, first on the adjacent property, then on mine. He said that he was looking for dandelion greens. The first time, he was standing at the end of the driveway just at the hour when I closed off the drive with a draped chain. I talked a moment with the man as he was not a stranger to me, and at the end of our conversation we shook hands, the normal gesture of respect.

On our second meeting when we again shook hands, his fingers tickled my palm. I thought, is it possible that he is using this schoolboy's gesture on me? Aurelio said that definitely it was. The third time the man came around I closed up the house and didn't speak to him, and I had Aurelio (in the role of my *amministratore*) tell the man that he was not welcome on my property. With reports of just such actions as these, my reputation as unavailable had certainly been circulated around town.

Little by little I was learning from Aurelio more and more the Tuscan way of life. One of the first matters of importance had to do with finances. Anything involving my money was a private affair. I had to be not only thriftier, Aurelio taught, but had to keep track on paper the amount of time any workman spent on the job at Il Poggetto. When it came time to pay either Gattone or a subcontractor, such as Michele, the man with the bulldozer and part-time diviner, I had to go over each item and compare notes. I was never to accept the total of a bill; the workers knew this convention and expected to subtract certain expenditures, often that had been padded into the bill in the first place. This was what Ciro had bawled me out about in front of the workmen several months earlier. But Aurelio explained himself and how and why this was customary; Ciro had simply made a scene, leaving me mortified.

On the other hand, I was never to fall into debt by accepting a gift or favor from anyone. Ciro had always been one to take whatever was offered to him, whether it was food, wine, or a favor such as someone running an errand for him. Aurelio came by the house one day and cut a huge pile of wild fennel to take to a friend. He was going to have to ask this friend for a small favor and wanted to pay the man back even before asking. The wild fennel was for the man's rabbits. Reciprocation was the key to avoid becoming indebted.

The first person with whom I wanted to get out of debt was Raffaella. I had sent her a commission for having found and bought Il Poggetto for me, but as she had continued to help (if that is the appropriate word) after my arrival on the scene, I was indebted to her. My job, then, became that of doing as much as possible for her and not letting her do anything for me. If she brought me roses from her garden, I would have some crème caramel for her to take back home with her. If I picked up a loaf of bread in town for her, she sent her leftover dinner home with me. Aurelio said indignantly, "Tell her you don't want her garbage." She gave me a pair of her middle son's faded black jeans. "You can cut them down to fit," she rationalized. It got to the point that we were giving and taking constantly, but I was determined.

Most of all I paid her back by supervising her house in her absence and in handing over house keys to English tenants during the summer months. The delivery of the keys turned out to be a euphemism for "do the cleaning when the paid domestic doesn't show up." There were times when my presence saved the day, such as when tenants arrived unexpectedly and found no one to greet them and the house a wreck. Raffaella, unbeknownst to me, had given the rental agent my phone number, and he called, blaming me for the confusion. "What do I know? I'm only her neighbor," I defended when he bawled me out. But I helped get the house in minimal order by discarding the trash and putting Raffaella's bedclothes in her closet. The renters, being English, took the mess in their stride, especially when the agent told them their rent would be halved.

Then I dog-sat various times for her three cute but not housebroken dogs at my house, and gave Raffaella my hospitality at times when her house was let. I would have done these things in any case, but the idea that I was getting out of her debt made me all the more willing to do them.

Aurelio had an aversion to Raffaella from the beginning. She was "bossy, arrogant, and talked too much," he said. When he saw how she pushed me around, he could hardly resist telling her off.

Finally Raffaella and I reached a point of no return. First she was offended when I began asserting my rights. For example, I denied her permission to cut down a tree that was on my property. Then we had the never-ending arguments over the town water problem. She more than anyone else became the instigator of gossip about me. She even told my sister-in-law Gina that I had a lover, then admitted to me that she had said it. We were in my car together: "I told Gina how difficult Ciro had become, that he behaves rudely to everyone. Then I told her that you have a lover, one of your workmen. I didn't mention names . . . " Gina, of course, told Ciro, but he didn't believe her. But the two women's meddling caused Ciro much unhappiness in the next three years. He didn't want to know the real situation. In the end

Raffaella and I stopped speaking – nothing less than a big relief to me. I had rid myself of a demanding husband only to find an equally difficult woman in his place – and she couldn't play the piano! Without the two of them in my life I could mature in my role as woman, property owner, and Italian citizen.

22. *AMORE, AMORE*

Although divorce had been legal in Italy for fewer than twenty years, extramarital affairs had existed for as long as matrimony. Italians accepted these *avventure* on the part of their spouses. The double standard prevailed: men were expected to have affairs through the years – to fool around was considered natural. Their wives, in most cases, could get away with extramarital relationships, too, but these were less easily tolerated. At a certain point a woman went from being a *brava donna*, a good woman, to being a *troia*, a sow, and with that lost her dignity and the respect of the community. It was not so much that the people feared damnation in hell for their lustful relationships, as it was their concern to walk with the head held high among their fellow citizens. On the matter of sexual adventures, the Church had not held up a high standard. How many popes in the past were fathers of illegitimate children, not to mention how many cardinals, bishops, and local priests had given in to carnal temptation?

The eighteen-year-old son of a friend of mine opened his heart to me on two or three occasions when we happened to meet. He said that as a boy he idolized his father, but that now he was disillusioned and unable to forgive his father for a "grave error." The young man had heard that his father was having an affair. Such an ongoing relationship, as opposed to casual sex, posed a threat to the family, meant a commitment to an outsider, and suggested a scandal. "Everyone does it," he said, "and everyone pretends it doesn't exist." He explained why he wanted to confide in me. "I chose you, Signora, because you are of a certain class and weren't born yesterday." But in fact I had very little exposure to the manner in which the people dealt with extramarital affairs. "Remember," he warned, "you are my bank vault; this is between you and me." He had proof of his accusations. He felt that his father was being disrespectful to the mother and that if she were to discover what was going on or if the worst happened – if the father left her for the other woman – "Mamma would die, I know it." She would die of humiliation, of embarrassment, more than out of pain in losing her husband to another.

This upset young man was Aurelio's son. The "other woman," obviously, was thought to be someone else, not me. I told him to concentrate more on his father's qualities and not to dwell on the "error." I never told Aurelio about his son's and my talks.

Tuscans in particular are known for their keen sense of humor, their ability to joke under even the most dismal circumstances. The subject of cuckolding is a main topic of conversation and teasing. The word for horns is *corna*, so the cuckold is referred to as *cornuto/a*. The gesture of the horns, the index and little fingers raised on one hand, is used to fend off evil spirits if the fingers tap some surface: if directed towards another person, the gesture signifies an insult. They said that if you directed the sign of the *corna* at an impertinent gypsy, she would recoil in horror.

So it was that men teasingly call each other "*Cornuto*". If a woman had had a lot of *avventure*, it was said of her, "She's seen more of them than a urinal has." If a child of a married couple resembled a man who was not the husband of its mother, in private the husband was jokingly referred to as the child's uncle.

A young *birichina* (spirited) married woman in a nearby town was having an *avventura* with a curly-haired truck driver. He would pass by her second-floor apartment and watch for the prearranged signals: if a white pillowcase were hanging from the clothesline on the woman's balcony, her husband was at home. No pillowcase on the line meant the coast was clear. The clothesline was supported by a cane pole.

One evening when she was alone, she saw her lover approaching on foot to her apartment house. Despite the all-clear signal, he was being cautious. The woman went on her balcony and sang out to her lover:

"*Vieni, vieni, è giunto il momento, il figlio è a letto, il maiale è dentro.*"

("Come, come, the moment is now, my son is in bed, the pig is inside.")

Another time the cane pole and, thus, the pillowcase had been blown down by the wind, giving her lover the impression she was alone when, in fact, she wasn't. Hearing her lover ascend the stairs to her apartment, she sang out as if singing a lullaby to her baby:

"*E' stato il vento a buttar' giù la canna, bimbo fa la nanna, il babbo vuol dormi'*"

("It was the wind that blew down the cane pole, baby go night-night, your father wants to sleep.")

A part of everyday life, these love affairs lasted a week, two years, or a lifetime. Discretion was the code word and was practiced always.

23. AVE MARIA

It had been nearly twenty years since my experience playing organ, and when don Paolo approached me with the idea of playing for Mass during the extra summer service, I got enthusiastic. The instrument I was to play was a two-manual pipe organ built just after World War II. It was in need of extensive repairs; many of the pipes had gone out of tune, and various stops didn't function. Mice had done their best to chew up the many pieces of leather used to connect inner workings. Still, I felt honored to play in the historic Church of San Francesco, the church of the priest who had blessed my house, and to participate in the community. I had no trouble with the hymns, as they were all familiar to me; now, though, they were sung in Italian.

To assist me was the church beadle, a tenor of sorts named Franco. He was an older man, thin and toothy, and he sang as though he had studied voice in a funeral parlor. He couldn't read music and had no particular talent, but his passion to serve God earned him the position of church soloist. He also managed to alienate anyone else who showed interest in singing. When Franco wasn't singing, he was talking, and he savored the opportunity of teaching me how music should be played in the Church of San Francesco in Sarteano. He was a fan of Ciro's, and after making numerous so-called improvements to a setting of the Ave Maria that my husband had composed, Franco added that piece to his repertoire.

Don Paolo understood my frustration and told me to pay no attention to him. But paying no attention to Franco was like ignoring a whining three-year-old. My enjoyment of playing for Mass outweighed my annoyance. After all, my playing season lasted only four months.

One Sunday morning, arriving twenty minutes before Mass, I found the church bedecked with flowers and in last-minute preparations for a wedding which I assumed would take place that afternoon. Instead, don Paolo greeted me with, "This morning we have a wedding!" I didn't have the music to the traditional Wagner "Wedding March," and I could no longer play it from memory, so I played the often-used Purcell "Trumpet Voluntary." The bride and groom seemed surprisingly unemotional at this high point of their lives. They were a couple well into their twenties and probably had been engaged for over ten years. All went smoothly during the Mass. No one from the wedding party spoke to me either before or after the ceremony. Some time later when I met the aunt of the groom, I told her that I had played the organ and sung for the wedding. "Oh," she said surprised, "I thought it was recorded music." There were two other weddings that summer, and don Paolo saw to it that I was given advance notice and that I got paid for my services.

It was during the period that I played organ that I met Lino. Lino was of an age somewhere between boy and man. He was fairly tall and husky and with a light beard. His large brown eyes had a questioning expression, and his aquiline nose made him look intellectual. I knew that Lino had no friends his own age; he was always out and about and always alone. He seemed neither to attend school nor have a job.

One Sunday Lino came back behind the altar where Franco and I were preparing for Mass. Franco spoke to him as if to a little boy and Lino did not respond, but he understood what was said to him. He wanted to be in charge of pushing the large red button that turned the organ on and off. He had done it before, and I certainly didn't mind giving him this pleasure. He remained quiet during the service, paying attention to his job. The organ got turned off before the homily, then on again, off at another point, then on for communion and off after the postlude, all to save on electricity.

Franco and I were singing a duet during communion, so that meant I had both hands, both feet, my voice, and Franco all going at once. When the music ended, I made a face to express my relief. Lino saw it and responded with a hearty laugh that resounded through the church.

Franco couldn't explain to me what Lino's problem was: "He's just like that," he dismissed the subject. Another person told me Lino was a deaf-mute. Lino returned only one other time to push the red button, but he always recognized me when he saw me in town, and he would greet me with a big smile.

Several Sundays later when I emerged from church into the splendid sunshine, I could see that an exciting event was going on. A long parade of antique cars driven by their upper class owners was passing through Sarteano on its way to somewhere important. Accompanying the parade were several plainclothes officials, as well as the local police, who helped keep the parade moving and local traffic halted. Lino was there and decided to take charge in his own way. Unnoticed by the busy officials, he began directing the traffic. He whistled and gesticulated with such authority that no driver doubted his instructions.

When Lino called out to a woman driver, "No, Signora, you have to turn this way," I realized he was not a deaf-mute. I'll never know where those trusting drivers ended up, but Lino certainly got them to go in the direction he intended. He was another of Sarteano's *matti*, but perhaps he was not as crazy as people thought.

Being church organist lost its allure mostly because I was not paid. But more important than the money itself was what being paid represented: respect. I could hardly be critical of Franco's lack of musical education if I as a professional was willing to work with him gratis, so after my four-month obligation I left don Paolo to recite Mass unaccompanied by the organ.

I made stabs at trying to make a living as a musician in Sarteano, but they were largely unsuccessful. Out of eight beginning piano students, only one remained faithful beyond the first few months. The children were all sweet and polite, but taking piano lessons was viewed as a summer pastime. If, after ten lessons between June and August, I had not turned an eight-year-old child into an accomplished pianist, the child and his (or usually her) parents, grandmother, and aunt gave up. "Little Maria has lost the *fantasia*," they lamented. Somehow from the beginning the concepts of practicing and long-term commitment never hit home. In fact, short-term was their understanding as most of the children had no piano at home and practiced either at a neighbor's house or on a borrowed electronic keyboard.

No, if I wanted to get back into a career, I would have needed to go outside Sarteano, perhaps to Arezzo or Siena, or, with real ambition, travel to Rome or Milan. But as Aurelio would say, "Why go looking for trouble?" This time it was I who had "lost the fantasy" – not that I didn't keep up my piano practice. I was like an understudy waiting to go on, but somehow I was not willing to call on musical acquaintances to help me get going. It wasn't laziness; it was an unwillingness to give up the work, the solitude and, most of all, the peace of my home.

One successful experience was with an almost-grown girl who wanted to study voice with me. Mirella was interested in all kinds of music and played guitar quite well. She willingly learned Monteverdi, Caccini, and bel canto arias, as well as Cole Porter, George Gershwin, and spirituals. By the time she left to go to college in Rome, she had a vast repertoire of songs and a devoted friend in me.

My first Easter alone, I was invited to her parents' house for brunch, so I dressed in my conservative Republican suit and drove into town. My hosts were a local architect and his wife, who was the middle-school principal. Most of the twenty other guests were older than I and were comfortably familiar friends of each other. I felt homesick and lonely, totally out of the conversation, though my hostess tried to include me by introducing me to the others individually. It was my first social event as a single, and I was so accustomed to being Ciro's companion that all I could do was talk about him and about our life together. As I talked I thought of how Ciro would be critical of my mistakes in Italian and that made me shy. As I tried to describe our duo-piano team and our musical projects, the polite listeners slowly moved away towards an old friend.

The food perked me up. In the rustic dining room a long refectory table was set up as a buffet. Set on the antique white tablecloth, were some eggs don Paolo had blessed; both green and ripe olives in brine; piquant salami from Sicily; and cool, soft cheeses. There were cheese-flavored bread and a delicate cake made with rose water and another cake made with candied fruit and in the shape of a dove, the *colomba*. At the end of the buffet were the traditional chocolate eggs. The red and white local wines were pure and light, but I drank very conservatively so as not to be labeled a typical American drunken *ubriacona*.

Most of the other guests were in town for the holidays and had come from Florence or Rome. Some had weekend houses in Sarteano, and a few of the men fit the role of country gentlemen, running farms with olive groves and vineyards. The Tuscan sense of humor saved the day for me, for I discovered that teasing got a good reaction from the others. It wasn't appropriate to joke like the farmers, of course, but the idea was basically the same. Instead of saying, as a *contadino* might, "You're just like parsley, always in the middle of things," I could teasingly admonish the man taking a second slice of cake about his cholesterol level. Instead of calling out "*Cornuto!*" I could smilingly call a Florentine by the familiar nickname of *becero* (boor). I had learned the nuances of the language by now. I was very appreciative at having been included in the festive brunch, but it was a relief to get back home, back to the familiarity of Il Poggetto.

Aurelio supported me in any project I chose. In most cases, he could see that supporting me meant leaving me alone to accomplish the project. But about working in Sarteano, he did not encourage me. He had not changed his opinion that I would be unappreciated locally. He knew the mentality of the people and realized that I would be taken advantage of as much as possible.

When I was discouraged about my professional life, Aurelio saw to it that I kept busy. There were always new projects and plenty of work at Il Poggetto. Whereas I had seen the property as a charming country cottage with a lovely garden, Aurelio went about turning it back into a farm.

One morning Aurelio brought a rooster and three hens to join Puffi and me. I wasted no time in naming them: Rooster, Speckle, Piebald, and Blacky. That was a mistake. With names attached to them, each one became an individual, almost a pet; when it came time to eat one of them, I was left with the sensation of eating a friend. When in the spring baby chicks hatched, I left them unnamed, and though they were fun to watch as they roamed free, I came to think of them primarily as a food source. I was not capable of wringing any necks, but once that deed was done, I had no qualms about plucking and cleaning Sunday dinner. The fact that the eggs and chickens were superior in flavor to store-processed was incontestable: just ask the fox who had managed to dine occasionally on one of the hens.

24. *BASTARDINA*

My goal since coming here had been to become Tuscan as much as I could, to accept and apply (even if I didn't always understand or approve of) the mores, the lifestyle, and the people. Especially after Ciro left, I cooked Italian, dressed Italian, and hung my bed linens out the window to air. In decorating the house I adopted the traditional Tuscan style with its simplicity and charm. I had worked hard at learning Italian and had avoided making friends with other Americans or English in the area. When Gianmarco offered to introduce me to fellow Americans, I said, "No, I didn't come here to meet Americans." In town I would see Americans or Brits, always paired up with each other, rarely socializing with Italians. I could never hope to be a true Tuscan; my American accent came through, my basic foundations were too different. But Aurelio teasingly called me *bastardina*, an almost-native. On other occasions he would call me *americana* with derision when he disapproved of something I said or did. If I smiled at a man I had just met or talked about something considered too personal, I was *americana*. To Aurelio, Americans on the whole were too rich, too friendly, and too gullible.

A lovely young woman in her early twenties, ,hter of local farmers, worked in one of the hardware .es. To me she was a great beauty, a Liz Taylor at the time of "National Velvet." One day I asked her if she were engaged. "No, Signora, I'll be the last one to get married," she said. When I asked Aurelio why she didn't have a boyfriend, he said, "Did you see those crooked legs? Who would want to be stuck with her! Besides, what were you doing asking her about her personal life? *Americana!*"

Fai la tua, learning to mind my own business and disdain gossip, became my way of life. Aurelio said that in Sarteano men were worse than the women when it came to gossip. "If someone spits," he claimed, "the whole town knows it before it hits the ground."

I was not without friends. Certain people's company was pure pleasure. As soon as I saw Aurelio drive up the road with his parents, for example, I knew I was in for a good time.

After sixty years of marriage, Gino and Immacolata were fondly sarcastic with one another. She would say, "Gino, it's time we went home." He would respond, "Why, because you can't bawl me out in front of the Signora? Give me a few more minutes' peace." Once, when we were all sitting outside, I apologized for the dirt on the lawn chairs. "Oh yes, with my delicate dress I must be careful," teased Immacolata, dressed in a worn cotton housedress and with a bandana on her head. It was the simple, folksy humor that reminded me of my grandparents in Indiana.

Immacolata would send some of her cooking by way of Aurelio. He would at times collect snails on the property after a rain, purge them for three days in a container with corn meal, then Immacolata would cook them in tomato sauce with herbs. Since the snails had come from my property, she felt responsible to give me some to eat. Aurelio gave me her recipe for *ragù* (meat sauce). The secret ingredient was to add a beef marrow bone to give the sauce rich flavor. Several times she sent a *ciambellone*, a Tuscan breakfast cake made in a Bundt pan. The next time she and Gino came to see me, I asked her for the recipe: "Four eggs well beaten with a lemon rind and four spoonfuls of oil. Add three *etti* (an Italian measure) of sugar, flour till it looks right, and a glass of milk. Last add an envelope of leavening. Oil and flour the pan and cook it over a low flame for one hour." "Don't you bake it in the oven?" I asked. "Oh, my oven hasn't worked in years, so I just cook it on top of the stove," she shrugged.

Aurelio phoned late one bleak afternoon. "*Babbo* is in the hospital. He's had a stroke. *Ha su' anima per i denti.* (He's got his soul by his teeth.) I have to stay with him all night until he's better." When I asked, "May I come to see him?" "Any time you want," he replied. Aurelio's father Gino had had a series of strokes; because of his illness, I had visited him in the hospital a couple of times before. This time, I could see he was on the mend when he couldn't resist laughing at his toothless roommate who was trying to chew his lunch.

Italy offered me the adventure of socialized medicine. Each citizen, including me now, was given a choice from among several general practitioners in town who then became that doctor's patient. There were private clinics, and specialists such as gynecologists were not necessarily under the State system but practiced privately. Affluent Italians went to Switzerland or France for their health care, especially if surgery was called for.

To go to the doctor in Sarteano, I did just that: go. There were no appointments, no nurses nor receptionists, no bill to pay! If the waiting room was full, the patients kept track of who went after whom; and as one left the doctor's office, the next one would enter. Usually things ran smoothly, and the average visit was about six minutes.

Often a patient needed to see the doctor only to renew a prescription.

There were no forms to fill out and no records were on file, as each patient was responsible for keeping his own receipts, written second opinions, and x-rays, and must present them if and when pertinent.

My doctor, Dottor` Vigano`, was in his thirties – attractive but not handsome – and highly dedicated. If he saw a patient on the street, he would go out of his way to greet that person.

During office hours the doctor was aware that there were others in the waiting room, but he never made a patient feel the need to rush. Once I took nearly twenty minutes of his time, but when I went back through the waiting room, the others looked at me more with curiosity than impatience. Stares of disapproval greeted the pharmaceutical salesman who appeared during office hours, but usually he, too, took only a few minutes of the doctor's time.

Doctors did make house calls: a fee for that service was charged, the amount left to the doctor's discretion. Being a *signora americana,* I was expected to have the doctor come to me rather than wait my turn among the *contadini* in the nondescript waiting room. That was not my style, and eventually my presence was taken for granted.

In the waiting room the older women sat in a row, their legs wide apart, long skirts covering their knees ("Let the air get in where it's needed most," their mothers taught.) They thought it necessary to pass the time by complaining. They complained, of course, about their health, but also about their husbands' health and about getting old. They brought up the name of a recently deceased relative or friend. (When a name was preceded by *po'ero* (poor), it meant that the person was dead.) The younger women had learned to sit with their legs crossed and often wore jeans. These women talked about their children and school. None talked about anything that did not have to do directly with themselves. No one would say, "I read yesterday that a scientist has discovered the secret of long life, and we will live to be 120 years old." First of all, no one would have read the news; second, if told of this discovery, they would have responded, "With all my troubles I certainly don't want to live that long!" Anything that didn't directly concern these people didn't exist for them, or at least had no importance. *"Non m'importa un bel niente"* they said. And why should they "give a damn," as the phrase might be translated. They were doing their best to get through life without suffering hunger, cold, or scandal. Their goal in life was not happiness, as that was considered unattainable. Dottor' Vigano', a native Sarteanan who studied medicine in Siena, returned to his hometown to practice. He said, "I like these people; they are simple."

Previous generations saved money not for themselves, but for their children. Not any more: now, people saved for their old age and physical needs because they knew they could not rely on their children to take care of them. Since three generations living together was the norm, everyone saved money. Mamma and Babbo both worked while Grandma babysat and did the cooking. (Usually *po'ero* Grandpa died long before Grandma.)

Gino had to go back to the hospital. To get to his room, I climbed five flights of stairs. The hospital had an elevator, but only the really feeble gave in to using it. I was nervous about going to see Gino because I didn't know him that well. Once I got to his room I found Aurelio there and knew I could relax.

Gino was sitting at a tiny Formica table: he had got up to eat. All the plates and cutlery in the hospital were plastic, so Aurelio had brought from home a linen place mat, a glass, and stainless steel cutlery plus a china plate. "They're treated like pigs here," he said with a grimace. But the nurses and other personnel were friendly and courteous, despite having to work under less than optimal conditions. Gino shared a room with two other men, both of whom were elderly, but no one was on an IV or hooked up to any kind of machine. The beds were normal twin-size, not automated hospital beds. There were no privacy curtains, no telephone, no television, not even straight chairs for the visitors. Along one wall were three closet/lockers with keys, one for each patient's personal belongings.

Because of a lack of personnel, traditionally a family member helped the patients at mealtime. Often a husband or wife kept vigil with the spouse all night. There were no call buttons; and to get to the bathroom, the patient (if ambulatory!) had to walk down the hall.

Sarteano's hospital had fewer services to offer every year, but it did not share with other Italian hospitals the problem of being overcrowded to the extent that patients were left lying in their beds along the corridors. Gino didn't complain; but like all patients, he was eager to go home.

Government institutions, including health care, were run on a national level. Local government had practically no power, so individuals had no rights; they were lost in the shuffle. Government workers could not be fired, whether or not they did their jobs, so inefficiency, absenteeism and indifference reigned along with *bustarelle* (extortion) and endlessly complicated bureaucracy.

Locally if people were asked who their congressperson was, they wouldn't know. They wouldn't really care, because they voted for their party, not the individual candidate. No one expected to be represented in government; once in power, the politician did what he wanted. It was assumed that most politicians were crooks, but Italy was clamping down and trying to improve its

208

image before the European Community. A negative image could hurt international trade and all-important tourism.

The campers who arrived in Sarteano from other countries in their European versions of Winnebagos were usually upper middle class, educated people; most of them spoke at least a few words of Italian. They were by and large nice families, quiet and neat. They dressed for the heat and for camping, wearing shorts, tank tops, and floppy sandals, making them easily recognizable. In the evening they would get cleaned up; and if there were a concert or art exhibit in town, they were the first to attend and appreciate the cultural event.

Tourism was Sarteano's main industry, even if the campers were not big spenders. In Chianciano, the spa town twenty minutes' drive away, the locals were as spoiled as their rich customers. The visitors were demanding. If a plate of pasta was not served *al dente*, it was sent back to the kitchen. Behind the scenes, the fresh replacement was spit into by the waiter before he smilingly served his complaining customer. In Sarteano, though, the prevailing attitude was that the customer is always right, and courtesy and a desire to please were the aim of the host townspeople.

I felt that I had been accepted in town when the merchants began giving me a knowing look while they waited on a foreigner who was struggling in sign language to describe what he needed. Patient eyes would signal me, "Ah, *questi stranieri* . . . " (Ah, these foreigners), and I was grateful that clearly I was not considered part of that group.

25. HOME TO STAY

Without Ciro in residence I began feeling more at home. I was no longer tagging along with him in town, and I dealt with the bank tellers, post office clerks, and grocers on my own. Mine was a different manner and attitude than Ciro's as I tried to behave like a small-town Tuscan. Because the merchants were getting used to my presence and accepted me, I felt I belonged. Now I, too, could tease gruff Felice about being "happy." I was no longer a new curiosity in town and enjoyed seeing the recently arrived naïve foreigners who had replaced me in the townspeople's interests.

Two basic Tuscan characteristics, *arrangiarsi* and *furbizia*, became recognizable to me in others, even though I couldn't bring myself to use them. Arrangiarsi was pretty much just survival of the fittest. It was no wonder that Tuscans, and Italians in general, were known for their cunning, their loyalty to those close to them, and their lack of trust in outsiders and the unknown. *"Non ti fidare,"* trust nothing and no one, was their motto. As the Dutch philosopher Spinoza wrote, "The preservation of one's own life and the fulfillment of one's functions are in themselves ethical."

Out of the indifference, inefficiency, and illegal goings-on in government grew arrangiarsi, to arrange oneself. It meant getting what you wanted by any available means, legal or not, and getting away with it. Tax evasion was an example. Most people evaded paying at least a portion of their income tax, largely by not giving their customers an official receipt. Work was done *al nero*, all cash, or with two receipts drawn up, one with the amount declared to the government, another handwritten for the customer with the amount actually paid. The customer would never denounce the person with whom he was dealing as both would end up in trouble and with a large penalty to pay. *Arrangiarsi* was a concept difficult for me. I was ingenuous and unsuspecting – *americana*. It took several experiences of *arrangiarsi* in action to convince me that it was the accepted and necessary way of life here.

The vineyard workers next door had always been friendly with me, but not too chummy. Sometimes I stopped to talk with the four or five of them working in the last rows of vines by my driveway. We made expected banal comments about the weather, this year's crop of grapes, and the state of my olive trees. Once one of the men kindly changed a flat tire on my old Fiat; the car was in the carport. I gave him a pack of American cigarettes so as not to be in his debt.

Puffi got to know the workers, but still barked when they came close to the property line. One day a part-time workman, an older man, had joined the others, and Puffi barked as threateningly as she could in her high-pitched voice. "Be careful," I called out from my side of the property, "she's ferocious!" "I'm ferocious, too!" the man called back. With this kind of harmless repartee with the *operai*, I had no reason to suspect them of being true masters of *arrangiarsi*.

A few months later I decided it would be a good investment to enlarge my property by about an acre of land. Aurelio was enthusiastic about putting in a dog run for his dogs and fencing in space for chickens. The land came from a larger parcel an absentee landlord had for sale. The piece edged on the south side of my property and gave me a tiny wood and several rows of grapevines, the rows being part of a much bigger vineyard. This vineyard had nothing to do with the one where the men worked; that was on the opposite side of my property.

After the purchase was made, I met up with the vineyard workers as they trimmed the vines near my house. The head worker began asking me casually about my new property. I told him that I had bought the woods, but offered no other information. He wanted to know the price of the rest of the vineyard parcel, so I told him who was handling the real estate. He hinted at whether or not I planned to build on the property, knowing that legally I couldn't; I said no. He asked other indirect questions, but I had learned to recognize the technique of *arrangiarsi* so gave away no information. It occurred to me that the owner and boss of this workman might have been interested in the other vineyard.

The next day Aurelio was able to tell me that it was not the vineyard owners who were interested in the parcel, but the son of the worker who had interrogated me. The man had been pumping me to see if I had been able to get a lower price than that quoted his son. He sought any information that would help in negotiating the deal, but I had not given away anything.

Arrangiarsi included being able to get information from sources and put that information to use to help get what was wanted. But it was important not to give out information at the same time that you were gathering it. Ask questions; don't answer them. "*Io mi arrangio,*" was the response to the questions how did you do that, find that, buy that for so little. It meant through intrigue and cunning the project was accomplished.

213

Here is another example of how *arrangiarsi* could work. Signor X buys the entire vineyard parcel, declaring for tax purposes that he paid a fraction of the actual cost and paying the seller in cash the difference. Then Signor X builds a barn on the new property, digging up an Etruscan tomb in the process underneath the structure. The Etruscan loot is sold on the black market. The barn, a legal structure, gets approved by the building code board, then is turned into a guest house, an illegal structure, and is let to foreigners in the summer without declaring that income. All this would be normal *arrangiarsi*. It is based, of course, on a person's unscrupulous lies.

The Guardia di Finanza is a special branch of law enforcement for tax evaders. This state-run finance police force made surprise visits to shops and offices, demanding to see the ledgers and account books. Many irregularities were overlooked by these special policemen if they were offered enough in the way of *bustarella*. A member of this force, for example, arrested a seven-year-old boy in Rome because he did not possess the receipt for a 75-cent bag of popcorn he had just purchased in a bar. The boy's father paid the equivalent of a $30 fine; the merchant paid $250 for the offense. Left laughing were the citizens who got away with millions of *lire* in tax evasion every year.

Honesty was considered a *vergogna*, shameful, and *furbizia* or cleverness, including the know-how of arrangiarsi, was an important attribute in everyday dealings. If a person was not *furbo*, which assumed an ability to get around the law, then he was *scemo*, a fool. Honesty was ridiculed.

Raffaella thought she knew how to be *furba*. She reveled in trying to put one over on others. To my satisfaction her *furbizia* got squelched by the locals whom she considered too unsophisticated to handle her. Just as she expected to influence the Communist committee and

214

its head to give me a building permit for my ground floor, she felt certain that she could haggle, cajole, or charm to get her way. Her rationalizations made no sense to anyone except herself, and the townspeople all complained about her.

Hidden in the trees on her property, Raffaella began building a two-story house without a permit, which she knew she couldn't do legally. When the authorities discovered the structure, probably reported by our common neighbor Bardini, they ordered her to tear it down. Instead, she went ahead with the roof, sure that she could *arrangiarsi* her way around the law. She managed to stall by paying a *condono*, a sort of legal *bustarella* that might have allowed her to get away with the building, depending on the whim of the council. But she was ordered again to tear down the unfinished structure. After two years of fighting the same council, she was left with an eyesore she can neither legally finish nor financially demolish. I already knew the aphorism, *"Più conosco gli uomini, più mi piacciono gli animali"* (The more I know men, the better I like animals.)

Puffi, of course, fit in the category of sublime human to me. We had been together for twelve years, and she had become my only live-in companion. She accompanied me nearly everywhere, riding on the back shelf of the car. When I couldn't take her with me, she was crestfallen and quietly, unintentionally, guilt-provoking. She made me keep a healthy routine: up not too late, a walk three times to the end of the driveway (at least), and a certain amount of time outside in good weather. She told me when it was lunchtime and when she thought she ought to have a bone. She warned me of trespassers, let me know when the fox was prowling around the chickens, and made me feel safe at night as she slept at the foot of my bed. I spoke Italian to her from the day we arrived in Italy, and she responded with adoring eyes and loving licks until she, too, understood the vocabulary. Puffi took to the country life immediately, but because she was allowed indoors she was considered a "dog of luxury" by the *operai* who were more familiar with hunting hounds.

I had known luxury too, but I was going from riches to rags. The house renovation took nearly all my capital, and there were still the projects of building a patio, installing an indoor staircase, and rebuilding the carport. The work would get done sooner or later, *pian piano*. Eventually, the fireplace did get repaired correctly. It wasn't necessary to dismantle it. Aurelio built an arch in the rear of the hearth, and the fireplace sent the smoke up the chimney. He was able to save its rustic exterior with that massive stone which represented my first real assertion with the workmen, that of putting the stone upright over the fireplace.

In finding Il Poggetto, I had found myself, my confident independence (a characteristic I had always valued but didn't have the courage to live), and had shed the negatives of superficiality, posturing, and conspicuous consumption. I developed the positives of a healthy lifestyle, serious intellectual pursuits, and an appreciation of the good people and their humor that surrounded me. Aurelio was with me, but through choice, not out of desperation on either of our parts. I felt whole in myself, and that meant I had more to give others, including Aurelio. When he told his parents about our relationship (something I could never have shared with mine), he explained how we felt by saying, "*Stiamo bene insieme*" (we go well together).

He had told me from the beginning that he would do all he could to help me, but that in return he wanted me to be here and to be his. He never pretended that he would divorce his wife. But if another man (Bedouin or not) were to come along for me, Aurelio said that he wanted out. He was right. I felt that Il Poggetto was

216

ours: without Aurelio it lost its significance for me. Every corner, every flower, reflected his work and proof of his love for me. I would be a fool to forsake this man; he had taken me from depression and desperation to glorious love and serenity.

As much as he wanted to see me confident and independent, these characteristics also made him feel threatened, worried that I no longer needed nor wanted him. One afternoon in the upstairs sitting room, Aurelio stood by me as if defeated. His posture, usually straight and strong, collapsed into that of an old man. His eyes stared at the tiled floor. "We are like Giotto with Cimabue," he said. "Your master has nothing more to teach you." I had never considered him my master, though perhaps I should have. I thought of him as an ally, a protector, a companion, and back in control of my life, I still wanted him with me.

To reassure him, I tried to laugh at his comparison of the two incomparable Italian painters, telling him that our relationship was much deeper than that of master and student. "I will never stop learning from you. I have built my world around you and what we share here, and that is all I want. I want no other man, no other life." He straightened up: "*Gioia!* Let's go take a walk in the *oliveto*."

If occasionally I felt alone and depressed, I would go outside, look at the view, and breathe in the fresh air. My problems didn't dissipate like the morning fog, but they did get put into perspective. Puffi and I were settled into our quiet routine that included Aurelio, certainly, but only with the limitations we both understood.

Sometimes a stranger would drive up to the house. I would meet him in the driveway, looking suspicious and unfriendly as a proper Tuscan should, only to hear him ask if the property were for sale. "*Nemmeno per sogno!*" (wouldn't dream of it) I would retort. Then in my mind I would hear Aurelio: "*Americana*! Why didn't you ask him how much he was offering?" But mine was a spontaneous and convincing reply that surprised even me, for you see, I was home to stay.

EPILOGUE

By Eden Tosi

REFLECTIONS

From the other side of the mirror.

Beneath the blue veins of this tale there is something else.
Evident is the force of destiny, of warning tides, the glances of the Tuscan
people, the sound of the word "Signora" implying respect and desire.
To this song the musician Susan Braggiotti abandons herself as if
pulled into an undercurrent.

But above all it is the fault of the light.
Of how the light falls in those parts: in Tuscany.
For us, people who come from other mists, from other harbors, we know
well that initial spell which always repeats itself, whether arriving by car or by foot, with eyes enraptured by the tremulous silver of an olive tree, the

warm red of the earth and graduated greens of the
vineyards in spring.

And we pause there, thinking of remaining alone for
awhile.

But don't believe in the sincerity of this book.
An operation, on the other hand, well-known as
impossible in an
autobiographical profile; an autobiography
firmly surrounding Susan.
In the precision of her story, yes, believe.
Things really happened this way.

Her way of story-telling describes the steps of a child,
like children making their way through the woods.
In this, believe.

It is a fact that Susan will die a child.

America.

For us America remains an exotic land.
A Tuscan from these parts allowed her his name.
Even so, even if belonging to us – like all things in this
world – it remains a faraway land.

The characters in this book are born amidst the humid
bricks of the houses, hunger scarcely known, the horse
manure collected from the street to fertilize the vegetable
garden. The bread and salt are not an uncertain
commodity. They were carefully counted, one by one,
grain by grain.
It was in the beginning of the era of plastic and the car
purchased in installments which for us at that time were
shameful. One already got along a little better.

In Sarteano's bars kids played billiards (or foosball) and we said "all'americana" who played brilliantly and imaginatively.

All the characters described herein met Susan, reverently, above all the humblest, noticed this her arrival from the other world.
Try also, dear readers, and you will find deep within Tuscany it is thus.

All the passages, the changes of scene between one chapter and the next, are born out of love.
On the other hand it is like this: if we remove the word "love" from the vocabulary, 1500 words disappear.
Scaffolding, cold Tramontana wind, bricks, cherry leaves, morning, glance, the blink of an eye, a 10,000 lire note, I'll stop to get you this evening, I'm coming up for coffee... all are synonymous with the word love.
Susan in describing the world surrounding Il Poggetto touches us all.
The protagonist herself here acts only for love.

She goes to Tuscany and stays because here she feels loved.
Just like all of us, we go where we are loved.

These are the same words uttered by Aurelio, minor hero of this story. Minor not because of a lack of intensity, this Prometheus with large hands, but because of destiny. Simple were his gifts, his walks with Susan, wine shared together.

Here there is nothing of Theseus, even if comparable with Ciro, strong hero of the chariot covered with flowers and garlands. Ciro, the sweetest monster of all her initial fantasies which with grace and feminine precision Susan Braggiotti paints.

Useless to leaf through the Etruscans of this land, this lofty passage of humanity, of how they put to rest their mortal dead. Or among the Romans of a distant Rome who can be seen from Il Poggetto.
No, this has nothing to do with myth.

Here, in this book by Susan Braggiotti, she deals with humanity.
That's all.

Modena, 23 April 2017
EDEN TOSI

Translated from the Italian by Susan Braggiotti

ACKNOWLEDGEMENTS

This novel began as a daily journal which I carefully wrote in Italian, hoping to improve my fluency in that beautiful language.

Now that a book has been born of that journal, I wish to thank some of the people whose support and editorial help were invaluable:

Valparaíso USA; Fernando Valverde, Eden Tosi, and Gordon McNeer have been unwavering in their confidence in this project and have helped on every level of the process.

Dr. Helena Talaya-Manso continues to be a source of inspiration and encouragement and convinced me that one can allow oneself to be a free spirit.

Dr. Clark W. Lemons gave hours of patient work on the final editing and offered wise advice on structure.

Beginning with the early drafts, Dr. Paula Buck helped correct what was disjunct writing. My brother David F. Snodgrass and his wife Mara Fisler Snodgrass provided constructive criticism and encouragement.

SUSAN BRAGGIOTTI
May 1, 2017